Empathy's Embrace
Guiding Your Child through the Transgender Spectrum

LIAM J. ADAIR, HHP

Copyright © 2023 by Liam J. Adair

Wholesome Healing Consultants, LLC
Houston, TX
https://www.whliam.com

All rights reserved. No part of this publication may be reproduced, stored in a retrieval system, or transmitted in any form or by any means, electronic, mechanical, photocopying, or otherwise, without the prior permission of the publisher.

Note to the Reader: *This book is intended as an informational guide. The remedies, approaches, and techniques described herein are meant to supplement, and not meant to be a substitute for, professional psychological care, medical care or treatment. They should not be used to treat a serious ailment without prior consultation with your qualified health care professional.*

First Printing: August 2023

Revised Printing: February 2025

10   9   8   7   6   5   4   3   2   1

A Library of Congress CIP (Cataloging-in-Publication) Number and copy of this book is available from the Library of Congress. Control Number:
LCCN: 2023917498

ISBN Hardcover: 979-8-9874637-4-1
ISBN EBook: 979-8-9874637-5-8

DEDICATION

To every soul journeying through the wonders of the human experience, seeking knowledge, understanding, and connection. To the inquisitive minds and tender hearts who strive to embrace the many expressions of gender and spirit. This book is dedicated to you. May its pages offer guidance, clarity, and a bridge to deeper empathy. And to the transgender, non-binary, and intersex individuals, whose courage, resilience, and authenticity inspire us all, may you forever find a world eager to understand and celebrate your truth.

CONTENTS

DEDICATION iii
CONTENTS v
INTRODUCTION vii
Chapter 1: The Basics: Introducing the Beautiful Medley of Gender 1
Chapter 2: The Harmony of Frequencies: Understanding Transgender Identities 5
Chapter 3: Understanding Gender: A Voyage Beyond the Binary 8
Chapter 4: A Peek Into Intersex Realities: Another "Parallel" Voyage Beyond the Binary ... 14
Chapter 5: Language Matters: Terms and Pronouns 26
Chapter 6: Historical Context: A Brief Look at Gender throughout Time 31
Chapter 7: The Complex Nature of Genetic Diversity: Understanding Chromosomes and the Prolific Nuance of Gender 42
Chapter 8: Answering the Question: Why Do People Transition? 51
Chapter 9: Answering the Question: Why Do People Detransition? 54
Chapter 10: Debunking Myths: Clearing up Lies & Common Misunderstandings ... 60
Chapter 11: Embracing Everyone: The Importance of Acceptance 69
Chapter 12: Recognizing Feelings: Empathy and the Transgender Experience ... 72
Chapter 13: Addressing Bullying: Standing Up for What's Right 75
Chapter 14: Role Models: Transgender Figures in Media and History 79
Chapter 15: Supporting Friends: How to be an Ally 93
Chapter 16: Families with Transgender Members: Love and Acceptance 99
Chapter 17: Finding Common Ground: Navigating Resistance within the Family ... 107
Chapter 18: Challenges and Triumphs: Real-life Scenarios 111
Chapter 19: Moving Forward: Cultivating a Respectful and Inclusive Tomorrow ... 115
CONCLUSION 121
ABOUT THE AUTHOR 123
Other Literary Works by: Liam J. Adair 124

INTRODUCTION

"Empathy's Embrace: Guiding Your Child through the Transgender Spectrum" is an inclusive exploration into the spectrum of gender identities, specifically focusing on introducing the concept of being transgender to young children between the ages of 5 and 12. At a time when children's natural curiosity blossoms, they often pose questions that adults find challenging to address. How do you explain the vast and varied world of gender identity to someone who's just begun to understand the basics of the world around them?

Our society has undergone significant evolution in its understanding of gender. Historically, many cultures recognized the existence of more than two genders. However, with time, rigid binary concepts of male and female became more dominant. It's crucial that our children grow up with a comprehensive and compassionate view of the world, understanding and respecting the myriad ways in which humans express their identities.

This book aims to bridge that knowledge gap. It provides age-appropriate explanations, personal anecdotes, historical contexts, and much more, allowing children to gain a foundational understanding of what it means to be transgender. With vivid illustrations, relatable scenarios, and simple language, "Understanding Transgender" will guide young readers (and their caregivers) through the diverse world of gender identity, emphasizing acceptance, empathy, and love.

As parents, guardians, educators, or simply concerned adults, we sometimes worry about saying the wrong thing or overcomplicating a topic. This guide provides you with the tools to approach these conversations with confidence. I have designed the chapters to include "Reflective Questions" for the guardians and the "Family Exercise" to be completed with the young ones and the adults. By educating our children early, we're laying the groundwork for a more accepting, understanding, and compassionate future generation.

"Empathy's Embrace: Guiding Your Child through the Transgender Spectrum " isn't just a book; it's an invitation. An invitation to journey into a world of self-discovery, empathy, and understanding. Within its pages, we illuminate the radiant spectrum of human experience, proving that our diversity is our strength.

Children are the most incredible learners. Their minds are like sponges, eager to soak up knowledge, free from the biases that sometimes limit adults. They marvel at the world's colors, sounds, and feelings with pure wonder. And just as they come to learn that there's more than one way to paint a picture or solve a puzzle, they can understand that there's more than one way to be a person.

In a garden, each flower blooms differently. Some might be roses, others daisies, and still others, tulips. Each flower has its unmatched beauty and special place in the garden. Similarly, every individual has their exclusive identity and place in the boundless garden of humanity. Through this book, we aim to celebrate the beauty of each identity, be it cisgender, transgender, non-binary, or any other way one might identify.

What makes this journey truly special is the shared stories. Real tales of courage, discovery, joy, and love. Narratives that demonstrate how every individual, no matter their gender identity, seeks acceptance, understanding, and a place to belong. By sharing these stories, we foster connection and build bridges of empathy.

Moreover, we realize that knowledge is most effective when shared in an environment of positivity and support. So, while we delve into complex concepts, our approach remains rooted in simplicity, warmth, and optimism. We emphasize the joy of discovery, the thrill of understanding, and the beauty of diversity.

In essence, this book is more than just words on pages. It's a collage of experiences, a chorus of voices, and a celebration of humanity in all its colorful forms. Let's set off on this enlightening journey together, fostering a future filled with respect, love, and boundless acceptance for all.

In Closing,

Let Us Be Present.

Let Us Be Of Light.

Let Us Be Of Love.

~Liam

Liam J. Adair

CHAPTER 1: THE BASICS: INTRODUCING THE BEAUTIFUL MEDLEY OF GENDER

As we begin this enlightening journey together, let us take a moment to center ourselves and embrace the wondrous diversity that makes up our human experience. Much like the expansive universe we live in, every individual is a distinct constellation of feelings, experiences, and identities. This chapter is a heartfelt invitation to dive deep into one of these facets: our understanding of gender.

When a new life enters this world, a proclamation is often heard: "It's a boy!" or "It's a girl!" This simple declaration, rooted in physical attributes, sets forth our earliest encounters with gender. But, as any seasoned traveler on life's spiritual journey knows, our true essence transcends the physical. Our gender identity is a dance between the soul and the universe, an intimate melody of how we perceive ourselves and wish to be seen.

Picture the boundless cosmos above. Stars, planets, galaxies, all coexisting in a harmonious dance. Each celestial body is unique, yet they all have their space, their light, and their significance. Similarly, while many individuals feel that their inner gender aligns with the physical attributes they were born with, termed "cisgender," others find their soul resonating to a different rhythm, identifying as "transgender." And then there are those whose spirits dance fluidly, identifying as "non-binary" or other wonderful expressions.

Think of our gender identity as the specific frequency at which our soul vibrates. Some might vibrate at the frequency of pink or blue, while others might resonate with a mix or an entirely different shade. There's no right or wrong, just different expressions of the same cosmic energy.

Isn't it marvelous to think of humanity as a grand orchestra, with each individual playing their one-of-a-kind note, creating a symphony of diverse identities? And just as every note is crucial to complete the melody, every gender identity adds depth, color, and beauty to the human experience.

According to the National Institute of Health, "understanding sex and gender is critical to understanding human health and disease.[1]"

Dimensions of Sex (Biological Variable) & Gender (Social and Cultural Variable)[2]

Table 1

SEX	GENDER
Anatomy	Identity
Physiology	Roles & Norms
Genetics	Relations
Hormones	Power

Within these pages, you will come to understand that an individual's sense of their own gender (for instance, as a woman, man, transman, transwoman, gender-diverse, gender fluid, or non-binary) is a deeply personal discovery that can evolve over their lifetime. This internal understanding of oneself might align with or diverge from the cultural norms and expectations traditionally associated with their biological characteristics. According to the Stanford Medicine Educational glossary[3], woman is a term used to "describe someone who self-identifies as a woman or as feminine based on what is important to them as an individual - including gender roles, behavior, expression, identity, and/or physiology" Note, that genital makeup is not deciding factor.

Dear reader, as we explore this realm of gender understanding, let us do so with open hearts and curious minds. Let's celebrate the infinite ways our souls choose to express themselves, understanding that every path is valid, every identity sacred. As we peel back layers of societal norms and expectations, we discover the boundless universe within, where love, acceptance, and understanding reign supreme.

---

[1] "What are Sex & Gender?" National Institute of Health (NIH). https://orwh.od.nih.gov/sex-gender

[2] Table 1. "Dimensions of Sex (Biological Variable) & Gender (Social and Cultural Variable". National Institute of Health (NIH). https://orwh.od.nih.gov/sex-gender

[3] "Woman." Stanford Medicine Educational Technology. https://mededucation.stanford.edu/glossary/woman/

Together, let's soar through this chapter and the ones that follow, spreading our wings of compassion, understanding, and spiritual connection. For in recognizing and celebrating our diversity, we come closer to the universal truth: We are all interconnected, radiant beams of the same divine light.

Ah, the magic of incarnation! The privilege of being on this Earth and having the opportunity to interact, learn, and grow. As spiritual and energetic beings having a human experience, our lives are a series of lessons and discoveries, of which understanding gender is but one of the many enlightening episodes.

Take a moment to marvel at the simplicity of nature. Observe a tree, with its incalculable leaves. No two leaves are exactly the same, each holding its characteristic shape, shade, and texture. Yet, all are vital for the tree's fullness and life. Similarly, our individual understandings and expressions of gender contribute to the diversity and vibrancy of our global family. Every identity, every expression, is a reflection of the universe's love for variety and distinctiveness.

When children play, they often do so without boundaries or fixed notions. In their games, a stick can be a sword, a wand, or even a musical instrument. Similarly, their understanding of self and identity is fluid, open, and untainted by societal constructs. It's from this place of purity and innocence that we, as guides and teachers, can introduce the concept of gender.

Now, imagine introducing a child to colors for the first time. You wouldn't just show them blue and pink and say, "That's all." You'd introduce them to the entire rainbow. In the same way, when talking about gender, it's vital to acknowledge and celebrate the entire spectrum. From cisgender to transgender, from binary to non-binary, and beyond – there's a plethora of ways individuals resonate with their inner truth.

As we dive deeper, remember that the essence of gender is not about labels but about authenticity. It's about honoring the inner voice that whispers (or sometimes shouts) about who we truly are. It's about recognizing and respecting that same voice in others, even if their tune is different from ours.

In our journey through life, we often find that true wisdom lies not in what we know, but in our capacity to understand, empathize, and love. As we navigate the spectrum of gender, it's essential to approach with the same ethos. Questions will arise, and that is understandable. Curiosity is a sign of an engaged and lively spirit. It's our duty, then, to foster a safe environment where these questions can be met with kindness, knowledge, and patience.

Reflective Questions

1. Think back to a time when you first learned about genders. What were some preconceived ideas you had, and how have they evolved over time?
2. How does the metaphor of a 'mosaic' help you understand the diversity of gender?
3. Can you think of any other natural or universal phenomena that demonstrate diversity and individuality like gender does?

Family Exercise: "Storytime of Diversity".

Objective: To understand and appreciate the variety that exists in nature, and relate it to gender diversity.

Instructions:

1. Collect a series of short stories or fables from various cultures that emphasize the theme of diversity, individuality, or acceptance.
2. Designate a family reading time where each member takes a turn reading a story aloud.
3. After each story, discuss the moral or theme of the story and how it relates to gender diversity.
4. Encourage children to create their own short stories that celebrate diversity.

Now, let's set forth with a heart full of love and a soul eager to understand. Remember, dear reader, we are not just learning about concepts and terms; we are learning about souls, about individual expressions of the Divine. And in that understanding, we find unity, compassion, and a deeper connection to all that is.

CHAPTER 2: THE HARMONY OF FREQUENCIES: UNDERSTANDING TRANSGENDER IDENTITIES

Life introduces us to melodies and frequencies that both challenge and enrich our energetic foundation. One such beautiful and reflective melody is the journey of transgender individuals. In this chapter, follow along on this heartfelt exploration of what it means to be transgender and how our narratives add depth and quality to our shared human existence.

Imagine, for a moment, a songbird perched upon a tree, pouring its heart out in song. But suppose this bird felt deep down that it sang with the voice of a different kind of bird, and its feathers felt unfamiliar. This dissonance, this feeling of a misalignment between the song it sings and the song it feels within, captures the essence of many transgender individuals' experiences.

Trans folks, much like many cisgender people, have an innate sense of their gender identity. However, their inner truth, the sacred song of their soul, might not align with the physical attributes they were born with. This realization can emerge as a gentle whisper or a roaring call, but it invariably speaks of a soul's longing to be seen, acknowledged, and loved in its authentic form.

I want is to journey together down the paths engrained with ancient wisdom. Across cultures and ages, there have been those who transcended the conventional boundaries of gender. They were revered as seers, shamans, and spiritual guides. Their incomparable experience of gender bestowed upon them insights and perceptions that enriched their communities. They were bridges, connecting realms, and their voices echoed truths that many could not perceive. Isn't it wondrous to think that the transgender narrative is as ancient as time itself?

But the modern journey of a transgender individual, like any existential spiritual journey, is not without its challenges. Imagine feeling the need to wear a mask every day, one that doesn't quite fit. Over time, this mask becomes heavy, burdensome. For many transgender individuals, embracing our true identity and setting-out on a transition journey, be it social, medical, or both, is akin to setting down that ill-fitting mask. It is a courageous act of self-love, a testament to the strength of the human spirit.

However, just as a budding flower requires nourishment, sunlight, and care, our transgender brothers, enbys, and sisters, too, need an environment of love, acceptance, and understanding. As co-travelers across the parallels of existence, it's our sacred duty to extend our support, to listen, and to learn.

Pause for a moment and tune inwards. Feel the heartbeat of existence, the rhythmic pulse that connects us all. Recognize that every heartbeat, every soul's song, holds value and purpose. In honoring and understanding the journey of transgender individuals, you are not just acknowledging a group; you are embracing the Divine in its many forms.

Reflective Questions:

1. Can you recall a time in your life when you felt different or out of place? How did that experience shape your understanding of yourself and others?
2. How do you think society's perceptions influence an individual's journey of self-discovery?
3. What are some positive affirmations or mantras that you can adopt to promote self-acceptance, both for yourself and others?

Family Exercise: "Tree of Self-Acceptance"

Objective: To visually represent and celebrate each family member's individual qualities and journey of self-discovery.

Instructions:

1. On a large sheet of paper or cardboard, draw a big tree with several branches but without leaves.
2. Cut out leaf shapes from colored papers. Each family member gets a

different color.

3. On each leaf, write down a quality, interest, or trait that represents you. It could be something you love about yourself or something you've come to accept.

4. Take turns discussing what you've written. After sharing, pin or glue your leaves onto the tree.

5. Over time, you can continue to add more leaves, representing growth in self-acceptance and understanding.

This exercise not only promotes individual self-acceptance but also fosters a supportive environment where every family member can appreciate and celebrate the diverse qualities of one another.

As we close this chapter, let's carry forth a renewed sense of wonder and reverence. Let us commit to being allies, listeners, and bearers of love. For in understanding and supporting the transgender narrative, you are, in essence, celebrating the beautiful spectrum of the human spirit.

CHAPTER 3: UNDERSTANDING GENDER: A VOYAGE BEYOND THE BINARY

In all its beauty and diversity, the human experience often defies the neat compartments and rigid boundaries society attempts to impose. Just as the colors of the rainbow seamlessly blend from one hue to the next, so too does the spectrum of gender identities that exist beyond the traditional binary concept of "male" and "female." At the center of this boundless space lies the non-binary identity, a term that holds immeasurable gender experiences and expressions that do not strictly align with conventional definitions.

The Fluidity of Gender

Throughout human history, societies across continents have borne witness to the multifaceted nature of gender. Our ancestors often held a more expansive view of gender, recognizing and even revering identities that existed beyond the binary framework. From the sworn virgins of the Balkans to the Hijra of South Asia, historical examples abound of cultures embracing the fluidity of gender. These historical precedents challenge the modern, often rigid, interpretations of gender, urging us to reconsider and reconnect with the vast spectrum of gender experiences.

In contemporary settings, the term "fluid" has become synonymous with identities that don't conform to fixed male or female categories. Gender-fluid individuals, for instance, may not identify strictly as male or female, and their gender expression may shift over time. This dynamic perspective on gender reflects the natural ebb and flow of human self-perception and experience, drawing a parallel to the ever-changing rhythms of nature itself.

According to the Human Rights Campaign, one of the leading LGBTQIA2S+ advocacy organizations, "gender-expansive" is a term that can broadly encompass the fluid spectrum of gender identities and expressions, including but not limited to non-binary, genderqueer, and gender-fluid. This terminology emphasizes the breadth and depth of the gender experience, pushing back against oversimplified and restrictive definitions.

However, the acceptance and understanding of gender fluidity aren't universal. Despite its deep historical roots and increasing contemporary recognition, many individuals and societies grapple with misconceptions and biases. These barriers, fueled by a lack of education and entrenched societal norms, often lead to the marginalization and discrimination of those who exist outside the binary system.

Yet, as the world becomes more interconnected and cultures intertwine, there's an optimistic shift towards more inclusive understandings of gender. Grassroots movements, community education, and the stories of gender-expansive individuals are paving the way for a future where the fluidity of gender is recognized, celebrated, and cherished for the splendid medley it adds to the human experience.

Non-Binary in the Modern World

In today's evolving social landscape, non-binary identities are becoming increasingly acknowledged; gaining both respect and damning dispositions. As our understanding of gender broadens, many are moving away from the limited confines of a binary gender system, which designates individuals as strictly male or female. Instead, people are made to recognize and embrace the reality that gender identity can exist beyond these two poles. The term "non-binary" acts as an umbrella, covering various gender identities.

Non-binary individuals might identify as having a gender that blends elements of both male and female, as having no gender, or as having a different gender entirely. The ways in which non-binary people express and understand their gender can vary widely, reflecting the large spectrum and fluid nature of gender identity. Physically, some might opt for a more androgynous presentation, others might express themselves in ways typically seen as masculine or feminine or choose presentations that fluctuate over time.

The World Professional Association for Transgender Health (WPATH) has been instrumental in pioneering research and medical guidelines for transgender and gender-diverse individuals. In one of WPATH's comprehensive research studies, the organization highlighted the importance of understanding and respecting non-binary identities. The study delved into the particular experiences and challenges faced by non-binary individuals, emphasizing the necessity of affirming healthcare and mental health support tailored to their specific needs.

Despite these advances in understanding and the increasing visibility of the non-binary community, challenges persist. Societal norms, ingrained biases, and lack of adequate representation in media and policy-making often lead to marginalization. This is further exacerbated by legal systems in many countries that don't recognize genders outside the binary, making it challenging for non-binary individuals to obtain identification documents that reflect their true selves.

Yet, the tide is gradually turning. Grassroots movements, advocacy by organizations like WPATH, and the lived experiences shared by non-binary individuals are challenging the status quo. As the world becomes more educated and empathetic, there's hope that non-binary identities will be fully acknowledged, respected, and celebrated as an integral part of the diverse human experience.

A Spiritual Perspective on Gender Fluidity

From my own spiritual understanding, gender is not just a physical or societal construct. For me, it represents a philosophical part of the soul's journey and the grand diversity of the universe. Understanding gender has always been about transcending societal expectations and diving deep into soulful introspection. Each individual, regardless of their gender identity, brings a unique energy, a vibration, which, in my eyes, adds to the universe's harmonic symphony.

In my teachings, I often speak about the interconnectedness of all beings. To truly embrace our authentic selves is a step toward spiritual enlightenment. Gender fluidity, non-binary identities, and all expressions of gender aren't just contemporary constructs; they're deeply spiritual, tracing their roots to the beginning of human understanding. My insights come from personal experiences, introspection, and years of connecting with others who are on similar paths.

The Brain's Perspective on Gender Fluidity

Some believe magic is just science that has yet to be confirmed. There were many medical conditions thought to have been curses and biblical plagues when humanity was facing extinction level viral infections and birth defects; in some cases. One of my blood-relatives believe that homosexuality is a curse performed by a witch that can be prayed away. This could not be further from the truth. Again, we are pushing against the poorly educated and ignorant. Historical and medical truth will help free humanity from the grips of trauma surrounding the discrimination towards the LGBTQIA2S+ community.

Science continues to affirm what transgender and non-binary people have always known in their hearts, gender is not simply assigned at birth, nor is it dictated by external appearance alone. The brain itself holds evidence of this truth. Studies on neuroanatomy have revealed that the brain structures of transgender individuals often align more closely with their gender identity rather than the sex they were assigned at birth.

One of the most studied areas in this regard is the bed nucleus of the stria terminalis (BNST), a region of the brain involved in processing emotions, stress responses, and aspects of identity. Research has shown that in transgender men, the BNST is comparable in size to that of cisgender men, while in transgender women, it mirrors the size of cisgender women[4]. This difference was not linked to hormone therapy, as the structural changes in the BNST appeared consistent regardless of whether the individual had undergone hormonal treatment. These variations were characterized in the specific region known to influence gender identity. Such findings suggest that gender identity is also deeply rooted in the brain's structure, rather than being a superficial or psychological choice.

For non-binary individuals, neuroimaging studies have begun to highlight variations that do not necessarily conform to a strict male or female pattern. This reinforces the reality that gender is not a rigid binary but a spectrum, with brain development reflecting the diversity of gender experiences.

Understanding these biological foundations can be life-affirming for transgender and non-binary individuals, offering scientific validation that their identities are not a deviation from nature, but rather a part of the natural diversity of human existence. This research also provides an opportunity for cisgender individuals to expand their understanding. If the human brain, the very organ that governs thought, emotion, and self-awareness, demonstrates

---

[4] Zhou JN, Hofman MA, Gooren LJ, Swaab DF. A sex difference in the human brain and its relation to transsexuality. Nature. 1995;378(6552):68-70. doi:10.1038/378068a0

gender diversity, then it becomes clear that transgender identities are not fabricated; they are intrinsic.

Acceptance begins with knowledge. Many people resist what they do not understand, but science offers clarity where ignorance once stood. For those who have been conditioned to see gender as fixed, these studies provide a tangible reason to rethink old beliefs. When presented with factual evidence, there is a choice: to remain in prejudice or to embrace truth with an open heart. The universe itself is built on balance and complexity, and human identity is no different. By seeking understanding rather than division, we align with a more energetically fluid, or spiritual order; one that welcomes all forms of existence, honors authenticity, and allows each being to live in harmony with their truest self.

Over the years, I've had the privilege of sharing my thoughts through writings, workshops, and heart-to-heart interactions. My aim has never been about personal accolades, but rather about creating a space for understanding and growth. A sentiment I often share is this: Within this endless multiverse, every soul finds its purpose, and every gender identity reflects a piece of the cosmos's elaborate wonder. We are, in fact, born of start dust.

Many have found solace in this spiritual viewpoint on gender, supported by science. It offers a space not just for acceptance but for celebration. By recognizing and honoring our gender identities as reflections of something divine, we find a deeper connection to the world around us and the mysteries it holds.

Reflective Questions:

1. How have your personal experiences shaped your understanding of gender?
2. Can you recall when you first encountered the concept of non-binary identities? What were your initial reactions or feelings?
3. How can you make space in your life to better understand and support non-binary individuals?

Family Exercise: Understanding the Fluidity

<u>Objective:</u> Explore the wide array of resources available to educate you and your family about gender fluid and non-binary insights.

<u>Instructions:</u>

1. Storytime: Read a children's book that features a non-binary character. Discuss the story, focusing on the feelings and experiences of the character.

   A. "Julian Is a Mermaid" by Jessica Love:
   While Jessica Love is not African American, her book is worth noting because it captures the spirit of self-acceptance and gender fluidity. It tells the story of Julián, a young boy who dreams of becoming a mermaid. The book beautifully explores themes of identity, acceptance, and the power of being seen.

   B. "I Am Perfectly Designed" by Karamo Brown and Jason "Rachel" Brown:
   Co-authored by Karamo Brown from "Queer Eye" and his son, this book is an ode to loving who you are, exactly as you are. While it doesn't directly address non-binary identities, it emphasizes self-acceptance and love.

2. Gender Spectrum Chart: Create a chart with a spectrum of colors. Discuss how each color might represent different gender identities and how they can blend together, much like the hues of a rainbow.

3. Interview Session: If possible and appropriate, speak with a non-binary individual willing to share their experiences. Listen with an open heart, and later discuss the conversation with your family, focusing on empathy, understanding, and acceptance.

This exercise aims to visually represent the concept of gender as a spectrum, allowing children to grasp the idea in a tangible, accessible manner.

As we conclude this chapter, may we always remember that every soul sings its own special song. Let us learn to cherish each note, each melody, and recognize the beauty of diversity within our multiverse.

CHAPTER 4: A PEEK INTO INTERSEX REALITIES: ANOTHER "PARALLEL" VOYAGE BEYOND THE BINARY

Insightful stories are abundant throughout our diverse human experiences. However, due to politics, prejudice, or lack of visibility, many stories often remain in the shadows; the stories of intersex people. Like the gentle whispers of leaves sharing tales, I invite you to lean in and listen closely.

Intersex and Transgender:

First and foremost, we must understand that being intersex is not synonymous with being transgender. Transgender relates to gender identity, where one's internal sense of being male, female, or another gender differs from their sex assigned at birth[5]. Intersex, on the other hand, is about biological variations where individuals might not fit typical definitions of what denotes a male or female body[6]. It's nature's gentle reminder of the many varied human experiences.

However, intersex children and teenagers face numerous challenges, including:

Medicalization: Decisions Are Made On Behalf of the Young Ones

---

[5] GLAAD's Tips for Allies of Transgender People. https://www.glaad.org/transgender/allies
[6] Intersex Society of North America's Definition. http://www.isna.org/faq/what_is_intersex

Unfortunately, many intersex children undergo surgeries without their knowledge or consent[7]. Imagine being reshaped without a say in the matter. It's a poignant reality many intersex individuals face. The well-meaning intent of doctors and parents to "normalize" intersex babies can lead them to decide the child's gender for them[8]. This seemingly well-intentioned intervention often carries emotional scars and feelings of being misplaced that can't ever be wholly undone.

Many intersex infants are whisked away for invasive procedures, with surgical instruments rewriting their stories before they even learn to speak their names. These procedures are carried out, after discussions between the guardians and surgeons, with the intention to assign a clear gender; to offer the child a "typical" life, free from potential societal biases or misunderstandings. Yet, in this quest for "normalcy", a deeper essence is often lost - the child's autonomy over their own body and the sanctity of their unaltered state.

The LGBTQIA2S+ community and, more specifically, the transgender and non-binary individuals, express strong discontent with these types of practices. We have experienced, first-hand, the horrors of such oversight and lack of respect shown for the rights and opinions of people regarding body autonomy, especially amongst intersex infants and children.

The repercussions of such medical interventions aren't just physical but extend into emotional and spiritual realms. As these children grow, they might grapple with feelings of being out of sync with their bodies, of being altered without a say. The psychological impact is intense, with many experiencing feelings of alienation, anger, and confusion. It becomes a journey of reconciling with a past decided by others, and often, the path to healing is long and winding.

Imagine the tender bud of a flower being reshaped just as it begins to bloom because its form doesn't align with what's considered "standard". In doing so, we might strip it of its extraordinary essence and beauty. Similarly, every intersex child carries a universe within, and to meddle without understanding is to risk obscuring their luminous potential. When given the choice, not every intersex person opts for gender confirmation surgery[9]. It's

---

[7] Human Rights Watch Report on Medically Unnecessary Surgeries. https://www.hrw.org/report/2017/07/25/i-want-be-nature-made-me/medically-unnecessary-surgeries-intersex-children-us

[8] UN Free & Equal Fact Sheet. https://www.unfe.org/system/unfe-65-Intersex_Factsheet_ENGLISH.pdf

[9] Intersex Awareness Day. https://intersexday.org/en/third-international-intersex-forum/

essential to note that gender identity is deeply personal, and while surgeries might feel right for some, others find solace in their unaltered state.

Societal Stigma: When Nature's Palette is Misunderstood

The realities of human existence are diverse, interconnected with an incalculable amount of shades and patterns, each adding depth and vibrancy to the whole. Yet, in a world that often seeks to neatly categorize and label its infinite complexities, intersex individuals find themselves at the intersections of misunderstanding and prejudice[10]. This is the challenge of societal stigma - a burden not borne from one's own identity, but from society's lens of viewing it.

Every culture has its stories, its folklore, and within them, a way of understanding the world. While diversity is celebrated in many forms - colors, flowers, stars, and landscapes - when it comes to the human spectrum, society tends to narrow its acceptance. Intersex individuals, with their particular biology, often find themselves outside these narrow definitions. They're perceived as anomalies rather than natural variations, and this results in feelings of isolation, invisibility, and marginalization.

This societal pressure fans outward, influencing families, communities, and institutions. Schools, places of worship, and community centers, spaces that are said to be inclusive, sometimes become theaters of whispered conversations and baseless judgments. It's in these everyday moments, these subtle glances, and hushed tones, that the weight of societal stigma presses down, shaping the self-worth and identity of intersex individuals.

The journey of understanding oneself in the face of societal disapproval is an extreme one. It's akin to a lone flower growing through a crack in a concrete pavement. Despite the weight and the shadows, it seeks the sun, displaying resilience and strength. Intersex individuals navigate this path daily, teaching us that true acceptance isn't just about tolerating difference but celebrating and embracing it.

Tackling daily life, every step, every twirl, every leap into the unknown becomes a testament to the indomitable spirit of those who, despite societal pressures, remain true to their essence and shine with unabashed authenticity.

Lack of Representation: Stories Waiting in the Wings

---

[10] InterACT: Advocates for Intersex Youth - Addressing Stigma. https://interactadvocates.org/intersex-insights/

In the books of history, where countless narratives shimmer and intertwine, intersex stories often remain eclipsed, waiting for their moment in the limelight. This lack of representation is not just about numbers or names; it's about the overpowering void one feels when one's essence, experiences, and truths are nowhere to be found in educational material, expressive art, media, literature, and daily discourse[11].

Consider, for a moment, the magic of seeing oneself in a story, of finding a mirror in a novel, film, or even a simple conversation. This reflection is validation, a silent nod from the universe saying, "You exist. You matter." For many intersex individuals, this magic is rare. Mainstream media often bypasses their personal narratives, either misrepresenting them or overlooking them entirely. This absence paints an incomplete picture of human diversity, leaving an echoing silence where vibrant voices should be.

But this isn't just about the stories left untold; it's about the implications of that silence. When young intersex children search for role models, for characters who feel the way they do, the scarcity is palpable. Similar to transgender identified children, the world seems to suggest that their experiences are not worthy of acknowledgment, or worse, that they're alone in their journey.

Yet, in this stillness, there's an undercurrent of change. As I referenced in one of my activity book, "LGBT Word Search", a new generation of artists, writers, and activists are emerging; building the narratives of intersex individuals with testimonies of authenticity and love. They are the storytellers and the dreamers, ensuring that no voice remains unheard, no tale untold.

As we, the seekers and sharers of wisdom, tread this spiritual path, it becomes our sacred duty to amplify these voices, to seek out these stories, and to ensure that the full history of intersex experiences finds its rightful place in our collective consciousness. For in every untold tale, there's a universe of understanding, waiting to be embraced.

Mental Health Struggles: The Silent Echoes of the Heart

Stepping forth on the path towards understanding the soul, it's important to recognize that our external world often mirrors our internal one. For many

---

[11] Human Rights Watch Report. "I Want to Be Like Nature Made Me". https://www.hrw.org/report/2017/07/25/i-want-be-nature-made-me/medically-unnecessary-surgeries-intersex-children-us

intersex individuals, the maze of self-discovery is made more complex by the weight of societal expectations, misunderstandings, and at times, the shadows of trauma[12].

The journey of self-acceptance is one that all souls undertake, but intersex individuals often find themselves navigating a path strewn with rare challenges. From the well-intentioned but misplaced concerns of loved ones to the broader societal stigmas, these experiences can give rise to feelings of isolation, confusion, and self-doubt. It's a poignant reminder that our mental landscapes are deeply intertwined with the world around us.

Research shows that intersex individuals are more susceptible to anxiety, depression, and other mental health concerns, not inherently, but due to the societal pressures and medical interventions they often endure. These struggles are not a testament to their resilience or strength, but rather a mirror reflecting the broader need for compassion, understanding, and authentic representation.

Yet, amid these challenges lies a radiant beacon of hope. The very resilience and strength that society so often overlooks in intersex individuals are the qualities that kindle hope, spark change, and inspire countless others. Their stories are not just tales of adversity but also of overcoming, of finding light in the darkest corners and of cultivating radiant joy from facets of sorrow.

As energy and spiritual beings, it's our divine calling to listen, to embrace, and to uplift. Let us walk alongside our intersex brothers and sisters, holding space for their stories, and in doing so, craft an exchange of understanding and unity that transcends the confines of the body and soul.

Education System Challenges: The Uncharted Paths of Learning

Can you vividly picture it, the classrooms and corridors of our educational system, where young minds are molded and futures forged? For many, these spaces were said to be sanctuaries of growth and enlightenment. But for our intersex siblings, these very spaces can sometimes become a complex terrain of misunderstanding, marginalization, and missed opportunities[13].

---

[12] InterACT Advocates for Intersex Youth: Addressing Mental Health.
https://interactadvocates.org/mental-health/

[13] InterACT Advocates for Intersex Youth: Intersex Affirming School Environments.
https://interactadvocates.org/education-system-challenges-for-intersex-youth/

Imagine the tender moments when the curriculum touches on human biology, reproduction, and genetics. For most students, these are standard lessons. But for the intersex child, it might be the glaring omission of their existence or the reduction of their experience to mere footnotes. Such omissions can unintentionally send a message, suggesting that their natural, divine variation is less valid, less understood, or less important.

Then there are school sports, locker rooms, and physical education. The binary structure of these activities often leaves little room for those who don't fit neatly into the conventional male or female categories. The process of team selections, uniforms, and even the simple act of changing clothes can become a source of anxiety and distress.

Moreover, school documentation, from enrollment forms to report cards, often doesn't accommodate non-binary or intersex identities. The very paperwork that should be a mere administrative detail becomes a poignant reminder of the system's unpreparedness to recognize and celebrate the spectrum of human existence.

Yet, just as the dawn follows the darkest night, there's a burgeoning awareness and growing movement to bring change. Progressive educators, compassionate students, and visionary policymakers are joining hands to rewrite the narrative. If we can incorporate intersex education into curriculums, reimagine inclusive sports programs, and adapt administrative protocols, we will lay a strengthened foundation for a more inclusive, empathetic, and holistic education system.

It is our collective spiritual endeavor to ensure that the light of understanding, acceptance, and love illuminates every classroom, every textbook, and every young soul searching for their place in this world.

The Right to Self-Determination: A Sacred Contract of Identity and Authenticity

Close your eyes, dear reader, and imagine a world where you wake up each day, not as the maestro of your own life, but as a wooden puppet, each move dictated by someone else's hand. It's a sobering thought, isn't it? For many intersex individuals, the struggle for self-determination, that inherent human right to steer one's own destiny, is not a philosophical pondering but a lived reality[14].

---

[14] InterACT Advocates for Intersex Youth: Advocacy for the Right to Self-determination.

From the very inception of life, many intersex children are met with a plethora of external voices attempting to define them. Decisions, often life-altering ones, are made on their behalf. Instead of being allowed the organic, sacred journey of self-discovery, their paths are frequently preordained by medical opinions, parental anxieties, and societal expectations. It's as if the songs of their souls are muted by the dissonance of external judgments.

But why, one might wonder, is the right to self-determination so deeply moving for our intersex siblings? It's because intertwined with this right is the ability to define one's own identity, to claim one's place in the universe, and to say, with both quietude and roaring confidence, "This is who I am."

Forced changes from outer influence often leads intersex individuals to grapple with feelings of powerlessness, loss, and a yearning to reclaim their authentic selves. Unfortunately, if those changes were surgical, they will not have the option to reclaim, but must learn to exist with the newly found understanding of their "new" normal. If you think about it, young ones are not always aware that an adjustment had been made until they reach the stage of puberty. Stepping into society as an adolescent, the world of peers, with the weight of a forced identity can cause a crisis. How can one begin to cope? Such instances call for the wholesome support of medical and psychological professionals and the LGBTQIA2S+ community alike.

Thankfully, the winds of change are rustling. A growing chorus of voices - intersex activists, allies, and enlightened souls - is rising, championing the cause of self-determination. This includes educating the parents and guardians of the intense effects of performing surgical procedures on young ones. They speak of a world where every intersex child is granted the grace to chart their own course, to dance to the beat of their heart, and to be the royals of their own sacred stories.

As we continue our shared journey of understanding, let us remember this: every individual, intersex or otherwise, is a universe unto themselves, deserving of the freedom to discover, define, and delight in their own divinity.

Legal Recognition: The Tale of Seeking Identity in a World of Paper and Ink

---

https://interactadvocates.org/right-to-self-determination-for-intersex-youth/

"What is in a name?"[15] More than mere labels, names help us navigate assuredly through a world of forms and structures to embrace our essence. For our intersex siblings, the quest for legal recognition becomes such a tale, a distressing interaction between their authentic self and the rigidity of human-made systems[16].

Imagine, if you will, beautiful garden with countless flowers, each nonconforming, each beautiful in its own right. Now envision a world that acknowledges only roses and tulips, leaving out the irises, daisies, and lilies. This is the landscape many intersex individuals navigate when it comes to legal recognition. Their distinct identities, adorned with shades and gradients, often find no reflection in the binary checkboxes of forms and documents.

The consequence of such oversight is extreme. Legal papers might seem to be mere sheets of paper, but in their ink lies the validation of existence, the right to belong, and the acknowledgment of one's truth. For intersex individuals, the lack of legal recognition often translates into challenges ranging from accessing appropriate healthcare to facing difficulties in employment and travel. I personally have countless airport stories of being sectioned off, subject to being "examined". It's akin to a bird, aware of its wings and the sky, but confined in a cage with no key in sight. You observe other soaring freely, only to have your cage opened after sundown, with a chain tethered to your foot.

However, as with all tales, this one, too, is evolving. Many intersex activists and allies are tirelessly working to transform this narrative; advocating for nuanced legal frameworks that honor the spectrum of human existence. Their call is clear: Recognize us for who we are, not just in spirit but in letter too.

As guardians of empathy and understanding, we must amplify this call. Let us remember that every individual is a melodic verse in the cosmic song, deserving to be sung, heard, and celebrated. In our shared pursuit of a more compassionate world, may we all strive to ensure that no one remains unseen or unacknowledged in the eyes of the law.

Identity and Community: The Soul's Quest for Belonging and Understanding

---

[15] Shakespear, William. (1597). "Romeo and Juliet.
[16] Intersex Human Rights Australia: Legal Recognition. https://ihra.org.au/18106/legal-recognition

You happen upon an ancient cave, walls adorned with crystals and gemstones - of diverse hues, patterns, and textures - observing each jewel symbolizing an individual's identity. Now, envision certain gems struggling to find their rightful place within this universal design, not because they lack vibrancy or importance, but because the frame's structure hasn't been adjusted to include them[17].

As Beings of this human experience, intersex individuals often face a deeply spiritual and existential challenge. The quest for identity becomes not just a personal exploration but also a search for a community that mirrors, understands, and embraces their own essence. As naturals as a lone wolf howling into the moonlit expanse, seeking others of its kind, intersex souls too *at times* reach out for validation and companionship in a world that may not always comprehend their truth. We are witnessing this act more and more amongst the cis-gender community members as well.

The Confluence of Narratives: Transgender and Intersex Surgical Data

To truly embrace humanity is an act of accepting that intersex and transgender individuals walk uncommon paths of their individual truths; each distinct and radiant in its own right. Yet, the stories of these two groups are sometimes intertwined in misleading ways, particularly by those with specific agendas.

Conservative activists have, on occasions, fused data related to surgeries performed on intersex infants with those concerning gender confirmation procedures for transgender individuals. This amalgamation often serves a narrative that suggests transgender children are being "forced" into surgeries, obscuring the distinct challenges and choices each community faces. Such narratives can be potent in stirring emotions and shaping public opinion, even when they're not anchored in reality.

It's crucial to understand that the medical procedures faced by intersex infants, often decided upon by parents and doctors without the child's consent, are a separate issue from the deeply personal and introspective journey transgender individuals undertake before opting for any medical interventions. The blending of these two narratives does a disservice to both communities, obscuring their distinct challenges and needs.

---

[17] Organisation Intersex International (OII) - Intersex Stories and Statistics from Australia. https://oii.org.au/

A notable example can be found in a publication by the Human Rights Campaign[18] which investigated the tactics of anti-LGBTQIA2S+ activists. This report highlights how certain factions conflate and misrepresent facts to further their narratives. Note that transgender and intersex individuals are estimated to make up approximately "1.7% of the population" in the U.S., "although some estimates may vary; depending on clinical definitions. Transgender individuals who may have undergone gender-affirming surgery may also have sex traits that do not conform to a single sex." [19]

Gender-affirming surgery studies will combine the data from cisgender, non-binary, and transgender patients. However, the lack of integrity some have skews the truth; but understand, anti-transgender organizations are aiming to mislead. The Harvard study has helped us recognize that 80% of chest augmentation surgeries are performed on cisgender men and 97% of chest reduction surgeries for children are performed on cisgender boys.

If an individual, identified as intersex at birth, underwent breast augmentation surgery, their data would be included in the study. If someone identified as cisgender male at birth underwent breast augmentation surgery, their data, too, would be included in the study. If someone identified as female at birth, but transitioned later in life and had breast reduction surgery, their information would also be included in this data report. Gender confirmation surgery refers to surgery performed to help someone's physical shell align with the image they hold regarding their ideal self (gender). The attack and harm towards transgender and non-binary people has nothing to do with surgeries nor medical treatment. It is because of their mere existence and it is fueled by misconceptions and false narratives.

This is the reason we have the constant drive to educate the LGBTQIA2S+ community. It promotes an environment of comfortable release and internal grounding that we desire to share with all. While some who face these challenges from society may cherish the solace of solitude at times, the beauty of community is undeniable. In a collective, we find reflections of ourselves, opportunities for growth, and the warmth of shared experiences. However, for many intersex individuals, such communities can be elusive. Mainstream narratives often overshadow their stories, leaving them in a liminal space, somewhere between the known and the yet-to-be-acknowledged.

---

[18] (HRC) (https://www.hrc.org/news/new-report-details-attacks-on-lgbt-youth-by-anti-lgbt-activists)

[19] Grimstad, F., Kremen, J., Streed, C. G. Jr., & Dalke, K. B. (2021). The health care of adults with differences in sex development or intersex traits is changing: Time to prepare clinicians and health systems. LGBT Health, 8(7), 439–443. https://doi.org/10.1089/lgbt.2021.0018

But, as with all stories of resilience and spirit, there are glimmers of hope. Slowly, the world is waking up to the harmonies sung by intersex voices. From grassroots initiatives and internal health studies, to global platforms, spaces are being carved out where intersex narratives are celebrated, shared, and uplifted. And within these sanctuaries, many find solace, understanding, and the joy of true belonging.

As seekers of light and understanding, it becomes our sacred duty to aid this awakening. By extending our hands and hearts, listening deeply, and forging pathways of inclusion, we can ensure that every soul finds its rightful place in the grand mosaic of existence.

Reflective Questions:

1. If you met someone who felt out of place because they were intersex, how would you comfort them using only your heart and words?

Family Exercise: Communicating Your Understanding of Intersex

Objective: Explore the different ways to communicate complex feelings, thoughts, and emotions in a supportive environment.

Instructions: Write and share meaningful letters aloud and discuss the feelings evoked.

Letter of Love and Support:
Imagine having an intersex friend. What loving and supportive words would you share with them? Each family member writes a letter filled with positivity and encouragement.

This exercise aims to visually represent the concept of gender as a spectrum, allowing children to grasp the idea in a tangible, accessible manner.

Society's understanding of intersex children and adults is clouded by misconceptions and prejudices. It's a reflection of our collective unfamiliarity, where difference is met with hesitancy. Intersex adults often recall memories of feeling isolated during their childhood because societal structures weren't built with their experiences in mind. The medical community, while striving for well-being, sometimes unintentionally adds layers of trauma by advocating surgeries without the individual's consent. This practice, deep-rooted in the medical world, has cascading effects on how society views and interacts with intersex individuals. Public discourse seldom accommodates the nuanced experiences of intersex people, leading to a sense of invisibility. However, the winds are changing, with more advocates bringing these stories to light.

In your journey to understanding and empathy, consider reaching out to intersex non-profit organizations for further insights (*list is not all inclusive*):

Texas:
InterACT Advocates for Intersex Youth. https://interactadvocates.org

Georgia: Organization Intersex International (OII-USA) https://oii-usa.org

Tennessee:
Intersex Initiative. http://www.ipdx.org

As spiritual seekers, our calling is to approach every story with an open heart, seeking understanding and clarity. By discerning the truth and recognizing the distinct paths of both intersex and transgender individuals, we honor their experiences and move closer to a world of genuine acceptance and love. May our journey always be guided by empathy and the earnest desire to understand the multi-faceted prisms of human existence.

CHAPTER 5: LANGUAGE MATTERS: TERMS AND PRONOUNS

Whether you assess your journey through life is spiritual, energetic, or material, we all agree that language is an important vessel through which we communicate our innermost truths, beliefs, and feelings. Treading along the path of enlightenment, we come to recognize the undeniable power of words. The magic of words. The authority of words. They do more than convey information; they touch souls, shape identities, and create realities. The world of language, in the context of gender diversity, doesn't have to be confusing. This chapter will help ease you into the identity labels known as pronouns.

The terms we use, the names we call, the pronouns we choose - all of these reflect our understanding, respect, and acceptance of the untold ways humans express their gender. To truly embody our spiritual beliefs in interconnectedness and universal love, we must first understand and then respect each individual's chosen language of identity.

Pronouns & Communication:

Pronouns are seemingly simple linguistic tools that replace names. Yet, in the complexity of the human identity, they take on great significance. The traditional pronouns "he" and "she" correspond to male and female gender identities. But, as we've learned, gender isn't strictly binary.

People who identify outside the binary might use "they/them" in a singular context, a usage that has historical precedence and is gaining acceptance in modern English. There are also neo-pronouns like "ze/zir" or "ey/em" that further reflect the diverse ways individuals perceive and express their gender.

When the uneducated express their discontent with pronouns, it reiterates their lack of understanding surrounding the functions of pronouns in language. We often hear those in opposition express that instead of respecting the identity of a transgender or non-binary person, they would rather remove pronouns from their vocabulary altogether; however, they might have an even more challenging time effectively communicating with others. Pronouns are essentially substitutes for nouns. This substitution is used both when you know the noun to which you are referring or unfamiliar with the subject. For example:

David is listening. He is listening.

The word "David" is the noun. The word "He" is the pronoun.

Michelle is listening. They are listening.

The word "Michelle" is the noun. The word "They" is the pronoun.

In the latter example, we did not use "he" nor "she" because we were not made aware of that person's gender. We do not lose any part of ourselves by referring to "Michelle" as "they". In fact, it helps us to avoid possibly misgendering "Michelle". This small act of "seeing" someone can help to reduce potentially stressful interactions.

Primary Pronoun Chart:

	I	Masculine	Feminine	Neutral	Ze/Zir	Hir	It	You
Subjective	I	He	She	They	Ze	Hir	It	You
Objective	I	Him	Her	Them	Zir	Hir	It	You
Possessive Adjective	My	His	Her	Their	Zir	Hir	Its	Your
Possessive Pronoun	Mine	His	Hers	Theirs	Zirs	Hirs	Its	Yours
Reflexive	Myself	Himself	Herself	Themselves	Zirself	Hirself	Itself	Yourself
Demonstrative	This	These	Those					That
Indefinite	Anyone	Everybody	Each	Some/None			What	
Interrogative	Who	Whose	Which					Whom
Reciprocal	Each other							One another

*Additional Pronouns: we, our, ourselves, ours.

The Deep Reverberation of Pronouns

Understanding and acceptance is essential to grasp the sincere essence of pronouns in our conversations and narratives. Open your mind and take part in an imaginative exercise: Picture yourself as a passionate poet whose soul is nourished by the rhythm and rhyme of words. Now, imagine the world around you consistently addressing you as a doctor. The mix-match, the sheer discordance of it, wouldn't just be a casual mistake; it would feel like an erosion of your true self.

The eloquent words of Black transgender activist and writer, Raquel Willis, resonate deeply here: "Our names and pronouns are the forefront of our humanity. Denying them is a major erasure." Just as Willis asserts, when society mistakenly or intentionally mislabels someone, it isn't a mere oversight. It's akin to suppressing the very essence of one's identity.

Spiritual practices from different cultures across the globe have long understood the power of names. Naming ceremonies are not mere traditional customs; they are poignant rites of passage. These moments crystallize the essence of an individual, offering blessings and embedding them within the community's shared narrative. Such ceremonies amplify the voice of the soul, allowing it to echo with clarity amidst the cosmos.

Concerning identity today, pronouns have assumed a similar sacredness. Raquel Willis, writer for the Auto Straddle, a digital publication for LGBTQIA+ rights stated, "We aren't the vessels of flesh that you continuously try to define for us. We aren't the insults, the wrong pronouns and the slurs you hurl towards us." Raquel's advocacy wasn't just about rights; it was about recognition, the rightful acknowledgment of one's existence.

When someone shares their pronouns, it is not a casual act. It's a personal revelation, a courageous step in asserting their existence in the universe. They are letting us into a sanctuary, revealing a sacred part of their soul's masterpiece. Our response, in using their correct pronouns, becomes an act of reverence, akin to the rituals performed during spiritual naming ceremonies.

To echo the sentiments of another prominent Black transgender activist, Janet Mock, "I am my best work—a series of road maps, reports, recipes, doodles, and prayers from the front lines." Each one of us is a masterpiece, a culmination of fathomless experiences and truths. By honoring someone's pronouns, we acknowledge and celebrate the distinctive artistry of their being, creating realities bonded together by threads of respect and understanding.

The Sacred Art of Attuned Listening:

Listening isn't just an auditory act—it's a spiritual endeavor, a bridge that connects souls. When we truly listen, we forge an energetic cord, entering a realm where words carry weight and silences are piercing. Along inaudible frequency waves, between heartbeats, in the pauses between words, the universe whispers its secrets.

When someone entrusts us with their pronouns, they are offering a fragment of their universe, a sacred insight into the constellation of their identity. An olive branch of trust is extended, revealing their foundational core. Just as in many holistic practices where we are taught to listen to the whispers of the earth, to the murmurs of the wind, and to the silent songs of the cosmos, it's imperative to bring that same reverence when listening to another's truth. To hear is human, to listen is divine. To act on what we've listened to is to dance with the spirits.

In our hurried lives, we often hear, but do we truly listen? When someone unfurls the inner-thoughts of their gender identity, do we pause and genuinely attune ourselves to the details of their narrative? Each of these moments of vulnerability add to their foundational relationship experiences. Do we readily accept them as they are, or do we create internal dialogue to manipulate their stories to fit our preconceived narratives?

There might be times when clarity eludes us, when the path is shrouded in uncertainty. In such moments, reaching out should become an act of tolerance and consideration. Asking someone, "What pronouns do you use?" isn't just about seeking information; it's about creating a space of safety, validation, and respect. In every question lies an intent; let yours always stem from love and the desire for understanding.

This act of inquiry is more than just etiquette—it's an affirmation. An affirmation that we see them, that we value their truth, and that we wish to walk beside them on their journey. It signifies a deeper commitment to not just knowing, but understanding and embracing.

As we deepen our understanding of language and its ties to identity, let's be ever-mindful of its power. Let's strive to use words that uplift, affirm, and honor. In doing so, we not only enhance our own spiritual journey but also contribute to a world where every individual feels seen, heard, and cherished.

Now, with this expanded understanding, let's take a moment to reflect on our relationship with language and its role in our lives.

Reflective Questions:

1. Recall a moment when someone got your name wrong. How did that feel?
2. Why do you think a small word like a pronoun can hold so much significance for someone?
3. How can we ensure we remember and use the correct pronouns for people around us?

Family Exercise: Pronoun Day

Objective: To foster empathy and understanding about the importance of pronouns.

Instructions:

1. Gather the family and create name badges for each member. However, instead of names, write down pronouns (including some beyond "he" and "she").
2. Distribute the badges randomly. Each family member will wear a badge that may or may not align with their gender identity.
3. Throughout the day, address each other only by these designated pronouns.
4. At the end of the day, regroup and discuss the experience. How did it feel? Was it confusing, validating, or perhaps enlightening?

The activity serves as a gentle reminder of the importance of pronouns and offers a firsthand experience of how it feels when one's gender identity is misaligned with societal expectations.

As we close this chapter, let's make a heartfelt commitment: to honor each soul's melody by calling it its true name and recognizing its authentic essence. Language, when used with care and respect, becomes a bridge connecting hearts and nurturing spirits.

With blessings of understanding and clarity, may you continue to walk the path of love and respect.

CHAPTER 6: HISTORICAL CONTEXT: A BRIEF LOOK AT GENDER THROUGHOUT TIME

The journey of understanding gender has evolved across cultures, societies, and eras. As humanity continued to progress, the numerous aspects of gender identity grew even more vibrant and complex. Through the eyes of a transgender spiritual-educator, embrace this diverse journey, tracing the footsteps of our ancestors and exploring the immeasurable ways in which gender has been perceived, silenced, all but eradicated, and also celebrated.

Two-Spirits: The Sacred Balance of North America's Indigenous People

The Indigenous cultures of North America have a deep understanding of gender, best encapsulated in the term 'Two-Spirits.' This term was birthed from an enhanced spiritual understanding that an individual could embody both masculine and feminine spirits. Far from being stigmatized, Two-Spirit individuals often held sacredly regarded positions in their communities, serving as healers, teachers, and spiritual leaders. You will see this as a common theme across all cultures that openly accepted their transgender and non-binary community members.

Their existence underscores a vital spiritual truth: gender is a fluid spectrum, not a binary. Many Native American tribes recognized this, valuing the Two-Spirit individuals for their otherworldly perspectives, balance, and ability to bridge the dual-nature and, often, contrasts of life. Tribes such as the Navajo, with their recognition of the 'nádleehi', and the Lakota, who honored 'Winkte', provide poignant examples of societies that embraced gender fluidity long before the term entered contemporary dialogue.

Sistergirls and Brotherboys: Embracing Fluidity Down-Under

Journeying to the sun-loved landscapes of Australia, we encounter another reflective testament to the ancient understanding of gender fluidity. The Aboriginal Australian people and Torres Strait Islanders refer to their transgender and non-binary community as 'Sistergirls' and 'Brotherboys'. For them, gender transition is not a recent concept; it is a timeless spiritual journey.

Sistergirls and Brotherboys, adhered to traditional societal roles within their tribal communities. Despite being depicted in Aboriginal drawings centuries ago, the transgender community was first acknowledged in the 2011 Australian census[20]. Currently, as many other transgender and non-binary communities across the globe, they face discrimination, scrutiny, and isolation from those within their familial and societal relationships.

The Bugis of the Indonesian Culture

The Bugis people, predominantly Muslim, intertwine their Islamic faith with traditional beliefs, creating a harmonious blend that guides their daily lives and understanding of the world. Their religion, a cornerstone of community life, fosters a space of respect and acceptance for diversity. The Bugis are one of four main ethnic groups of South Sulawesi, a slender peninsular region of the Sulawesi Island that stretches south towards the island of Flores in the Indonesian archipelago[21]. Showing the complexity and fruitfulness of gender identity beyond the binary, the Bugis people recognize five genders.

The Five Genders:

1. Calalai: recorded as biologically female at birth but live, dress, and work in society as male (generally identify as non-binary)
2. Calabai: recorded as biologically male at birth but live, dress, and work in society as female (generally identify as non-binary)

---

[20] Kerry, Stephen Craig. (2015). "Sistergirls/Brotherboys: The Status of Indigenous Transgender Australians." March 2015 International Journal of Transgenderism 15(3-4):173-186 DOI:10.1080/15532739.2014.995262. ResearchGate.net.

[21] Anderson, Mark. August 15, 2016. "Beyond Binary: Five Genders of the Bugis". Anthropology Gender Focus. Akkaduim College.

3. Oroane: recorded as biologically male at birth and live, dress, and work in society as male (generally identify as male)
4. Makkurai: recorded as biologically female at birth and live, dress, and work in society as female (generally identify as female)
5. Bissu: generally recorded as biologically ambiguous but live as embodiments of male, female, mortal, and deity combined (generally classified as intersex)

As reported by Anderson, Sharyn Graham Davies, the Associate Professor of New Zealand's Aukland University, compiled extensive ethnographic research into the Bugis' conceptions of gender. Over a fifteen month project, Davies observed that bissu embody aspects of all genders within them. She considers them beyond gender – 'meta-gender' or 'gender-transcendent'. Bissu's appearance may be androgynous or gender-ambiguous. As with many of the cultures we have studied, the gender fluidity is believed to invoke the bissu with spiritual powers. Bissu are highly regarded in society due to their interconnectedness with the spiritual and physical planes. As religious authorities, bissu coordinate the community's important ceremonies. "They heal the sick, officiate at weddings and bestow ritual blessings upon people in the community"[22]. Davies has observed the bissu at work, and describes complex rituals in which reverence for Allah is blended with shamanic trance, chanting and possession by spirits or deities (dewata).

Davies interviewed bissu Mariani. Mariani who described the duties and stressed the importance of bissu to the community and their practices. "… you must understand, neither a man nor a woman is powerful (sakti) enough to be possessed (disurupi) by dewata, and if you can't be possessed, then you're not bissu. It's the combination of woman and man, and human and dewata, that makes us bissu."

The Bugis' approach to gender is a testament to their nuanced understanding of identity, where each person's essence is acknowledged and celebrated.

India's Hijra Community

The Hijra community, often regarded as the "third gender" in India, holds a comprehensive and layered position within the subcontinent's populous cultural network. For centuries, the Hijras (hosting a range of individuals, including, transgender, intersex, and eunuchs) were historically well-regarded

---

[22] Anderson, Mark. August 15, 2016. "Beyond Binary: Five Genders of the Bugis". Anthropology Gender Focus. Akkaduim College.

but later ostracized. Ancient Hindu scriptures reveal that they possess the power to bless and curse, making their presence sought after during childbirth and weddings; where they bestow blessings for fertility and prosperity. At the same time, due to societal shifts and colonial legacies, they've also faced significant discrimination and have been pushed to the margins of society, often resorting to begging or sex work for survival.

Historically, the Hijra community's spiritual significance can be traced back to foundational texts of Hinduism. Legends from the Mahabharata and the Ramayana, ancient Indian epics, bear stories of Hijra characters that wielded significant influence. For example, the tale of Shikhandi from the Mahabharata depicts a character who played a vital role in the Kurukshetra war, and their story is intertwined with themes of gender fluidity and transformation. Such narratives, deeply embedded within the collective Indian psyche, underscore the underlying acceptance and recognition of gender diversity in ancient India.

However, the colonial period marked a dark chapter for the Hijras. From the late 1500's to the 1800's, British colonizers led a 300-year campaign of hate and murderous discrimination. With their rigid Victorian and religious morals, criminalized the Hijra community, leading to their systemic persecution. The legacy of this era lasted even post-independence, with the community facing continuous discrimination. But recent decades have witnessed a gradual shift. In 2014, India's Supreme Court officially recognized the Hijra community as the "third gender," paving the way for increased rights and acceptance. While challenges persist, the resilience and enduring cultural significance of the Hijras remain a testament to their indomitable spirit within the vivacity of Indian society.

Being Transgender in the Motherland (Africa)

Africa, a land vibrant with the echoes of ancient civilizations and deep-seated cultural histories. There once existed a paramount understanding and acceptance of gender diversity that predated many modern narratives. These communities, with intimate connections to the earth, the cosmos, and the spirit world, offer us lessons in acceptance, love, and the fluidity of existence. Historically, African societies have recognized more than the binary genders, embracing a spectrum of identities with honor and respect. From tribes of the savannas to the dense rainforests, there have been recorded instances of populations where gender was seen as a fluid concept, not confined by the colonial binary system.

One such example is found among the Yoruba people, where the concept of "Ayanmo" suggests that destiny is not fixed by gender at birth. The Yoruba, along with other tribes, have historically recognized the existence of individuals who embody both masculine and feminine spirits, showing that the spiritual essence of a person transcends physical form. These individuals often held significant roles within their communities, serving as mediators, healers, or custodians of sacred knowledge, bridging the mundane with the divine.

The Dagara people of West Africa held a similar belief, where gender and sexuality were viewed through a spiritual lens. Among the Dagara, it was shared that intersex, transgender, and non-gender conforming individuals were gatekeepers between the physical and spiritual worlds, blessed with the ability to see life from multiple perspectives. Their existence was presented as a vital part of the community energetic balance, contributing to the health and well-being of their villages.

Citizens of Western Africa in the Kingdom of Buganda, part of modern-day Uganda, recognized the existence of transgender individuals in their society. Historical records accounted for individuals who were assigned male at birth but lived their lives as women, fulfilling roles and duties traditionally reserved for women in Buganda society. As stated by artist and native of Uganda, Leilah Babirye, "many transgender women, whom we refer to as queens in the Kuchu Clan community,... love naming themselves after their favorite aunts, sisters, or women role models."[23] These individuals were not marginalized but rather accepted and integrated, showcasing a societal structure that honored a spectrum of gender identities.

The Mudoko Dako also held a respected place in their society. Originating from the Lango people of Uganda, the Mudoko Dako were described as individuals assigned male at birth who naturally embody both masculine and feminine energies. This blending of spirits transcended matters of social roles but was deeply intertwined with the spiritual practices of their community. Their recognition by the Lango was a testament to the understanding that they inherently viewed gender on a spectrum, a multitude of possibilities, rather than a fixed dichotomy. It highlighted the wisdom of the Lango people in embracing and valuing the multiplicity of human expression.

Similarly, in Madagascar, the Sakalava kingdom celebrated the "sekrata," individuals who combined male and female social roles and appearances. The sekrata were showed respect for their abilities as essential spiritual wellness

---

[23] Babirye, Leilah. 2022. "Ebika Bya ba Kuchu mu Buganda (Kuchu Clans of Buganda). Gordon Robichaux at 1464 West Temple Street Exhibition Venue

leaders, embodying traits and characteristics of both genders.

Unfortunately, as with the Indigenous Americans and the Hijras of India, following the introductions of the colonizers' Christianity, the African transgender community faced extreme prejudice and scrutiny. This led to many being disowned, assaulted, displaced, imprisoned, placed in concentration camps, or unalived.

Even still, in reflecting upon these historical data points, it is clear that the diversity of gender identity is not a new phenomenon, nor is it at odds with the whole of African cultural and spiritual practices. Instead, it is deeply embedded in the continent's gorgeous variety of life. These traditions remind us that every individual, regardless of their gender identity, holds a sacred place in the universe. They teach us the importance of embracing and celebrating the full spectrum of human experience.

As we move forward, let us carry with us the wisdom of Africa's ancestral teachings. Let us create spaces of understanding and acceptance, where every soul is free to express its true essence. In doing so, we honor not only the legacy of those who came before us but also pave the way for a world where love, in all its forms, is recognized as the ultimate truth.

Non-binary, No New Concept: The Jewish Talmud & the Eight Genders

The ancient Jewish teachings of the Talmud reveals customs, legal traditions, and understandings that have been shared for thousands of lifetimes[24]. Within these teachings, there lies the understanding that gender is not only fluid, it is also a vast constellation, where each star shines with its own light, stories, and truths, illuminating the endless night sky of human diversity.

The Eight Genders:

1. Nekevah: female
2. Zachar: male
3. Androgynos: having both male and female characteristics
4. Tumtum: lacking sexual characteristics
5. Aylonit hamah: identified female at birth but later naturally developing male characteristics

---

[24] Scheinermn, Rachel. (2024). "Gender & Sexuality: The Eight Genders in the Talmud". My Jewish Learing.

6. Aylonit adam: identified female at birth but later developing male characteristics through human intervention.
7. Sarishamah: identified male at birth but later naturally developing female characteristics
8. Saris adam: identified male at birth but later developing female characteristics through human intervention.

Mahu Healers: Historic Pillars of Hawaiian Tradition

The Mahu of Hawaii were highly respected within the cultural and spiritual landscape of the islands, symbolizing a spiritual nature of both male and female qualities that transcended conventional-western gender norms. Similar to the Two-Spirits of the Native Americans, they were recognized for their impactful roles beyond social and spiritual guidance. Mahu were sought after and celebrated for their exceptional healing abilities; embedded in ancient Hawaiian traditions. Both "Mahu in the Middle: The Hawaiian Knowledge of Intermediacy" and "The Power of the Steel-tipped Pen: Reconstructing Native Hawaiian Intellectual History" helps us to understand that their knowledge of herbal medicine, coupled with spiritual practices, allowed them to serve as healers within their communities, addressing both physical ailments and the people's spiritual well-being.

In their honor, the native Hawaiians placed four boulders on Waikiki beach over 500 years ago. This exhibit is named "The Healing Stones of Kapaemahu" as Kapaemahu was the leader of the four healers. In 1906 James Alapuna Harbottle Boyd wrote an excerpt in his manuscript entitled the "Tradition of the Wizard Stones of Ka-Pae-Mahu" in which stated the Hawaiian people loved the healers for their "tall stature, courteous ways and kindly manners" and their cures became famous across Oahu.

Hinaleimoana Wong-Kalu, a mahu who is a respected cultural practitioner and community leader was featured in the film "Kumo Hina" (co-directed by Dean Hamer and Joe Wilson). Wong-Kalu expressed that the mahu "were respected and honored because the people knew that their male and female duality made them even more powerful a healer." This deep-seated wisdom highlights the Mahu's crucial role in maintaining the health and balance of their communities.

The mahu's story was passed down orally, like all Hawaiian stories, until a written language was developed in the 1800s. However, with the arrival of colonizing Westerners and Christian missionaries, the Hawaiians who practiced traditional methods were tortured and persecuted. In 1893, the teaching of Hawaiian language in public schools was banned and also discouraged from being spoken in their personal dwellings until ultimately being lifted in 1987; 91-years later..

The acknowledgment of mahu and figures such as the traditional healers and Wong-Kalu, in Hawaiian society, underscores the importance of embracing diversity and recognizing the impactful contributions of all individuals, regardless of gender identity. Their roles in healing, education, and cultural preservation highlight the integral part they play in Hawaiian society, ensuring the continuation of a culture that values inclusivity, respect, and aloha.

Transgender History in the United States: An Unwavering Quest for Recognition and Rights

Turning our attention to the United States, the journey of transgender individuals stands as a testament to resilience, courage, and an unyielding quest for recognition. The U.S., a blended collective of cultures and identities, witnessed the emergence and evolution of transgender narratives in the midst of civil rights movements, cultural revolutions, and technological advancements.

Early accounts on the non-gender conforming community was documented by the courts in the 1620s. Thomas/Thomasine Hall, was brought before a Virginia Colony judge in 1629 because the town members, after repeatedly examining Hall's genitals, could not determine how Hall should be allowed to present themselves in public. It was legally decided that Hall would be forced to wear a "man's" breeches and "woman's" apron and cap. This legal decision only served to further reinforce the west's notion of the gender binary; denying Hall of their right to present as they desired. By today's terms, Hall would be considered intersex. However, it is important to stress that they would not be inherently labeled transgender nor non-binary. If they so choose, they could have identified as male or female as well.

In 1866, Francis Thompson, the first Black transgender woman to testify before congress, spoke of her harrowing experience during the Memphis Massacre. Thompson and her cis-gender friend, Lucy Smith, described the "SA" they and 3 other Black women endured at the hands of the white men who took part in destroying over 91 black-owned businesses, churches and other dwellings. Over 46 Black Americans were unalived during that massacre. Ten years later, Thompson was arrested and charged with being a "man dressed in women's clothing". While incarcerated, she suffered abuse at the hands of the prison staff and other inmates. Less than a year later, shortly after her release, Thompson passed away due to a bacterial infection she contracted while incarcerated.

In the early 20th century, transgender individuals often lived discreetly, navigating a society that barely acknowledged their existence. However, as the century progressed, the nascent cries for recognition grew louder. By the 1950s and 60s, pioneers like Christine Jorgensen brought the conversation into the mainstream, challenging society's understanding of gender and identity.

The Stonewall riots of 1969, a decisive moment in LGBTQIA2S+ history, further highlighted the pressing need for transgender rights. Led in part by brave transgender women of color like Marsha P. Johnson and Sylvia Rivera, this uprising marked the beginning of a more visible and organized fight for transgender and queer rights in the country.

As decades passed, the struggle persisted. From legal battles for gender marker changes on identification documents to the fight for healthcare rights and protection against discrimination, the U.S. transgender community, despite numerous challenges, continued its relentless march forward.

Cultural shifts, too, began to reflect more inclusivity. By the 21st century, transgender figures in media, arts, politics, and science started gaining recognition, bringing with them stories of triumph, heartache, determination, and hope. This gradual yet significant transformation in American society underscores the idea that understanding and acceptance, while often hard-won, are always possible.

Understanding this chapter of history is crucial. It provides context to the modern-day rights and protections transgender individuals in the U.S. have and highlights the sacrifices made to achieve them. The resilience of the transgender community in America serves as a beacon of hope, illuminating the path for future generations.

An Ever-Evolving Universe of Complex Energies

These historical glimpses into various cultures' understanding of gender elucidate a universal truth: gender diversity is as old as humanity itself. Each culture, in its special way, has acknowledged, shunned, destroyed, celebrated, or admired this diversity, weaving it into its spiritual fabric.

While contemporary conversations on gender might seem new, they are merely the latest gems in an age-old patch-work quilt. The wisdom of our ancestors calls out to us, urging us to embrace, understand, and respect the sacred melody of gender identities.

However, as with many aspects of indigenous and different cultures throughout history, the colonization and westernization of many parts of the world led to the suppression, erasure, or stigmatization of these traditional roles and those that walked that path. The global spread of certain religious or cultural beliefs often resulted in the sidelining, persecution, and needless unalivings of many transgender individuals. Yet, despite centuries of marginalization, the resilience of transgender figures across global contexts remains a testament to the enduring spirit of those who live authentically. Their stories are not just tales of survival but also of resistance, revival, and reclamation.

Becoming aware of how inclusive our transgender individuals were in their familial communities, I find solace, pride, and affirmation in these historical narratives. They remind us that our journey, while deeply personal, is also a collective experience. We walk a path that has been tread upon by countless souls before us, each contributing to the world-community of human understanding and compassion.

Reflective Questions:

1. How do these historical perspectives on gender challenge or affirm your current understanding?
2. What can we learn from the way ancient cultures embraced and integrated gender diversity?
3. How might recognizing the deep historical roots of gender diversity impact contemporary conversations on the topic?
4. How has the understanding of transgender rights in the U.S. evolved over the decades?
5. What challenges did transgender pioneers face, and how did their courage pave the way for future generations?
6. How can learning about the struggles and triumphs of the transgender community in the U.S. foster empathy and understanding?

This exercise provides not only a historical perspective but also a sense of gratitude and respect for those who fought for rights and recognition in the face of immense challenges.

Family Exercise: Timeline of Triumphs

Objective 1: To help families understand the diverse ways in which gender has been perceived across cultures and time.

Instructions:

1. Spread out a large world map on a table or the floor.
2. Place markers or stickers on the regions discussed (North America for Two-Spirit, Australia for Sistergirls and Brotherboys, and India for Hijras), etc.
3. As a family, discuss each region and its cultural understanding of gender. Use this as an opportunity to teach children about the splendor and diversity of global perspectives.
4. Encourage children to think of how these historical concepts can be applied in today's world, fostering understanding and acceptance.

Objective 2: To create a visual representation of the pivotal moments in U.S. transgender history, allowing families to recognize and appreciate the journey and struggles of the community.

Instructions:

1. Using a long strip of paper, mark it with decades from the 1900s onwards.
2. Together as a family, research and note down significant events in U.S. transgender history for each decade. Use colors, pictures, and keywords.
3. Discuss each event, ensuring children understand its significance.
4. Encourage discussions on how each event or personality contributed to the broader understanding and acceptance of transgender individuals.

In the symphony of existence, every note matters, every rhythm contributes, and every voice deserves to be heard. As we look back and honor the diverse ways our ancestors understood and celebrated gender, we pave the way for a future where every individual, regardless of their gender identity, feels seen, respected, and cherished.

Liam J. Adair

CHAPTER 7: THE COMPLEX NATURE OF GENETIC DIVERSITY: UNDERSTANDING CHROMOSOMES AND THE PROLIFIC NUANCE OF GENDER

The gentle hum of human existence is amplified throughout the multiverse, harmonizing the frequencies of science, personal stories, spirituality, and shared experiences. Within each of us, there's a microscopic universe, a realm where our DNA vibrates to unique frequencies, forming, directing, and projecting various aspects of who we are. Our chromosomes, particularly, play a role in determining what is traditionally termed as "biological sex". While XX and XY chromosomal patterns are widely recognized as female and male, nature's repertoire is more varied, echoing the abundance of life itself.

XX and XY:
These are the most commonly recognized chromosomal combinations, often aligning with "typical" female and male physiological presentations. However, along the human spectrum, both within and out of these categories, there are natural biological variations. For example, a study from the "Best Practice & Research Clinical Endocrinology & Metabolism" narrates the story of Mikey, a young child with XY chromosomes. Challenging common conventions, Mikey's journey offers insights into the intimate dance between chromosomes and gender identity.

Mikey's Radiant Journey with PMDS: Embracing Dualities

In our multidimensional existence, every individual is a single thread, weaving stories that resonate with lessons and love. Mikey's thread held a mystique that would only reveal its full colors with time. When Mikey arrived into this world, the universe celebrated not just the birth of a boy, but of a soul with a vital journey ahead.

At a tender age of seven, during a gentle twist in Mikey's path, the universe whispered its secret. Mikey was diagnosed with Persistent Müllerian duct syndrome (PMDS) (46,XY), a rare condition which meant that while they had the external presence of a male, inside, they bore the sacred chambers of female reproduction. The number 46 refers to the fact that Mikey has, the generally expected, 23-chromosome pairs. The great dance of life had intertwined both male and female aspects within Mikey, making them a true embodiment of life's dualities.

The spiritual beauty of PMDS is in its testament to the universe's infinite variations. While science attributes the condition to nuances in the AMH or AMHR2 genes, from a spiritual lens, it's a reminder of the limitless forms life can take[25]. Embracing their PMDS, Mikey found harmony within, transitioning to resonate more with their feminine energy and now identifies as female with she/her pronouns. With the unwavering love and support of her family, she set sail on this journey with grace and courage.

As the years flowed, Mikey experienced the divine blessing of pregnancy, further affirming the universe's wondrous design. Carrying life within her, she became a beacon of hope and testament to the miracles that lie beyond societal norms. Her pregnancy was not just about birthing a child but also birthing a new understanding of life's great possibilities.

Through Mikey's journey, we're reminded of the words of ancient sages - we are not just flesh and bone but spirits, ever-evolving and boundless. Mikey's story is a celestial reminder that we are more than our external selves, we are souls with boundless potential, and every path, no matter how seemingly insignificant, is sprinkled with stardust and divine purpose.

XXY (Klinefelter syndrome):

---

[25] Hughes, I. A. (2011). Disorders of sex development: A new definition and classification. Best Practice & Research Clinical Endocrinology & Metabolism, 25(2), 119-134.

This combination can lead to a spectrum of physical characteristics, often resulting in males with an extra X chromosome. However, because of the presence of the extra X chromosome, some physiological characteristics might differ from XY males.

Common physical traits associated with Klinefelter syndrome can include:
- Smaller testes and penis
- Reduced facial and body hair (compared to typical XY males)
- Enlarged breast tissue (gynecomastia)
- Lower testosterone levels, leading to reduced muscle mass and bone density

Despite these physiological differences, it's important to remember that Klinefelter syndrome doesn't necessarily influence gender identity. Many individuals with the syndrome identify as male, but as with anyone, gender identity can be diverse.

Ayden's Experience
Ayden's journey with Klinefelter syndrome began with speech delays and learning challenges[26]. After a diagnosis at age 10, his family embarked on a mission to understand and support his needs. His mother, Emily, became an advocate, creating support networks and raising awareness about the condition. Ayden, now a teenager, continues to navigate social and academic challenges with resilience, highlighting the importance of community and advocacy.

Aleksander Berezkin's Advocacy
Diagnosed with Klinefelter syndrome at 17, Aleksander faced societal stigma in Russia[27]. Embracing his identity, he became an intersex human rights activist, founding the Association of the Russian-Speaking Intersex. His work emphasizes the intersection of biology, identity, and human rights, advocating for acceptance and understanding.

XO (Turner syndrome):
Typically, individuals with Turner syndrome have a single X chromosome and no Y chromosome. These individuals are generally classified as female and have female external genitalia.

---

[26] Emily. (April 19, 2022). "Emily on Raising a Son with Klinefelter Syndrome". Healthy Male Australia. https://healthymale.org.au/real-stories/experience-parenting-mum-child-klinefelter-syndrome
[27] https://aleksanderberezkin.weebly.com/

However, many physiological characteristics can be associated with Turner syndrome, some of which relate to reproductive anatomy:

Underdeveloped ovaries (often called "streak ovaries") that are nonfunctional
- No menstrual cycle or onset of puberty without hormone treatments
- Short stature
- Webbed neck
- Broad chest and widely spaced nipples

Even though these individuals have female external genitalia, the underdevelopment or non-functionality of the ovaries often leads to infertility. Like anyone else, their gender identity is a personal aspect of who they are, and many with Turner syndrome identify as female or non-binary and can present as Asexual (having no sexual interest in other people; although, they may still be interested romantically). However, gender identity is a complex interplay of biology, identity, culture, and personal experience.

Peyton's Journey
Diagnosed at age 8, Peyton faced health challenges associated with Turner syndrome, including short stature and potential fertility issues[28]. With support from the Turner Syndrome Center at Cincinnati Children's Hospital, she received comprehensive care addressing her physical and emotional needs. Peyton's story underscores the importance of early diagnosis and specialized support in managing Turner syndrome.

Carlin's Story
Diagnosed at 3, Carlin is a verbally gifted child with a passion for science and art. Through comprehensive care and a supportive environment, she leads a happy, healthy life, demonstrating that with the right support, individuals with Turner syndrome can thrive[29].

XXX (Triple X syndrome):
Individuals with an XXX chromosome configuration have a condition

---

[28] Krummen, Lisa. Krummen, Peyton. (April 10, 2019). "Peyton's Story: Living with Turner Syndrome." Cincinnati Children's Hospital.
https://www.cincinnatichildrens.org/service/e/endocrinology/patient-stories/peyton-turner-syndrome
[29] Children's Hospital of Philadelphia. "Turner Syndrome Second Opinion: Carlin's Story".
https://www.chop.edu/stories/turner-syndrome-second-opinion-carlin-s-story

known as Trisomy X or Triple X syndrome. These individuals are phenotypically female, meaning they typically present with female external genitalia.

In many cases, females with Trisomy X have no significant physical differences from females with an XX chromosome configuration, and they may not even be aware that they have an additional X chromosome. However, some might have associated physical or developmental characteristics, which can include:

- Taller than average stature
- Learning disabilities or delays in speech and language development
- Behavioral and emotional difficulties
- Menstrual irregularities or early menopause

Despite these potential differences, the majority of XXX individuals live typical lives, have typical fertility, and might not ever realize they have this chromosomal variation unless they undergo chromosomal testing for some other reason. Their gender identity is usually female, but as with all people, individual experiences can vary.

> Heidi's daughter was diagnosed with Triple X syndrome, a condition where females have an extra X chromosome[30]. Despite initial concerns, Heidi found that her daughter could lead a healthy life with proper support. She emphasizes the importance of awareness and understanding, noting that many girls with Triple X syndrome can thrive with the right interventions.

XYY Syndrome:
Individuals with the one X and two Y chromosomal make-up are generally assigned male at birth. Occurring in approximately 1 out of every 1,000 assigned-male-at-birth-individuals, physically they are taller than average with some developmental differences. However, these differences do not prevent them from living fully active lives. Characteristics can include:

- Taller than average stature
- Normal fertility
- Possible mild delays in speech and language development

---

[30] "Heidi's Daughter has Triple X Syndrome and She Wants You to Know What It Is". https://myplanmanager.com.au/heidis-daughter-has-triple-x-syndrome

- Learning difficulties (especially reading)
- Behavioral challenges in some cases (impulsivity, attention difficulties (ADHD, ADD, Autism)
- Normal sexual developmental and identity

While early studies pathologized this condition, more recent research has affirmed that most individuals with XYY live healthy, productive lives. It is a naturally occurring variation, one of many that challenge the notion of a rigid binary biological framework.

> Steve, a man standing at 6'6", always felt different growing up. Despite being from an academically accomplished family, he faced challenges in school, often being misunderstood and labeled as immature. It wasn't until adulthood, during fertility investigations, that he discovered he had 47,XYY syndrome, a condition where males have an extra Y chromosome[31].
>
> Throughout his life, Steve grappled with low muscle tone, social difficulties, and learning challenges. These experiences, while daunting, didn't deter him. He pursued higher education, secured a fulfilling job as a Student Center Administrator at a university, and became a dedicated father. Steve's resilience and determination exemplify how individuals with 47,XYY can lead successful and meaningful lives.
>
> Beyond his personal achievements, Steve became an advocate, educating healthcare providers and parents about XYY syndrome. He emphasizes the importance of early diagnosis and holistic support, ensuring that individuals with chromosomal variations receive the understanding and resources they need to thrive.

XXYY (48,XXYY Syndrome):
This is a sex chromosome aneuploidy that occurs in about 1 in 18,000 to 40,000 assigned-male-at-birth individuals. Though it is classified under the umbrella of Klinefelter variants, XXYY presents with distinct social and cognitive patterns. Spiritually, these individuals often carry a uniquely sensitive vibration; energetically attuned and deeply perceptive. You will likely see these individuals lean towards careers in the Health and Wellness industry. Typical characteristics include:

- Taller than average height

---

[31] Genetic.Org. "What is XYY? Meet Steve and Find Out". https://genetic.org/what-is-xyy-steve

- Delays in speech and motor skills
- Learning disabilities and emotional regulation issues
- Possible infertility
- Low testosterone levels
- Possible presence of autism-like traits or ADHD symptoms
- Increased risk of anxiety and depression

One case presented by the Genetics Home Reference (now part of MedlinePlus) shared the story of an adolescent with XXYY who, through family therapy and early intervention, found empowerment in community and advocacy[32]. His family shifted their focus from "fixing" him to supporting his evolving identity, leading to deeper connection and confidence.

XXXY (48,XXXY Syndrome):

This chromosomal variation represents yet another reminder that identity cannot be reduced to biology alone. It's found in approximately 1 in every 50,000 assigned-male-at-birth individuals. Many with XXXY syndrome are non-verbal or experience communication challenges, but energetically, they often exhibit profound emotional sensitivity and connection. In spiritual terms, they often feel like old souls; soft, intuitive, and deeply in tune with energies beyond words. Beautifully represented, their typical characteristics could be:

- Developmental delays and intellectual disability (usually moderate)
- Hypotonia (low muscle tone, could lead to dystrophy or cerebral palsy)
- Distinct facial features and skeletal abnormalities in some cases
- Infertility
- Delayed speech and language acquisition
- Friendly and affectionate personality

In the documentary The Human Variome Project[33], a participant named Elijah, diagnosed with XXXY, shared his journey through alternative education and holistic therapy. His caregivers emphasized sound healing, breathwork, and movement to support his expression. Elijah's presence in their lives, they reported, shifted their

---

[32] National Library of Medicine. MedlinePlus Genetics: 48,XXYY Syndrome.
[33] Human Variome Project, Clinical Genetics Reports, 2018.

understanding of patience, love, and what it means to "listen" beyond verbal communication.

XXXXY (49, XXXXY Syndrome):
This syndrome is sometimes referred to as "Fraccaro Syndrome[34]," a rare form of sex chromosome aneuploidy with five total sex chromosomes. These individuals often require lifelong support but carry immense light into the lives of their caregivers. Their presence challenges the illusion of normalcy, inviting all who meet them to embody deeper compassion and patience.

A 2020 case study published in the American Journal of Medical Genetics[35] detailed the story of a boy named Mateo, who inspired his community through inclusion efforts at his local school. His parents, guided by both spiritual practice and medical insight, created a support network that combined traditional therapies with healing circles, storytelling, and nature-based rituals. His story became one of not just survival, but impact, showing how difference can be a guiding light for community transformation.

Within the educational sphere of archaeology, scientists have long aimed to ascertain the gender of skeletal remains. A research paper from the "Journal of Archaeological Science" elucidates that while certain skeletal features, like the pelvis, might hint at an individual's physiological sex, a comprehensive determination of gender from bones remains elusive[36]. Gender is an interrelated fusion of social identity, culture, and personal character.

To navigate the overarching terrains of genetics and gender, let me draw from the wisdom of Neil deGrasse Tyson: "The universe is under no obligation to make sense to you." Yet, in its infinite complexity, it offers glimpses of unbridled beauty and connection. Whether a being comes into the world with XXY, XYY, XXYY, XXXY, or any other variation, they are no less whole. They are no less sacred. They are no less deserving of dignity, autonomy, and support in whatever gendered or non-gendered path they resonate with. Our genetic tales remind us that we are, indeed, wondrously made, and each should be allowed to uniquely develop in to the Being that aligns with our most reassuring frequency. Through understanding and

---

[34] Johnson, E. et al. (2020). Clinical Profiles of Rare Sex Chromosome Aneuploidies. AJMG.
[35] Johnson, E. et al. (2020). Clinical Profiles of Rare Sex Chromosome Aneuploidies. AJMG.
[36] Evangelia Daskalaki, Cecilia Anderung, Louise Humphrey, Anders Götherström. "Further developments in molecular sex assignment: a blind test of 18th and 19th century human skeletons. Journal of Archaeological Science, Volume 38, Issue 6, 2011. Pages 1326-1330, ISSN 0305-4403, https://doi.org/10.1016/j.jas.2011.01.009.

empathy, we can cherish the melodies and harmonies within and around us.

Reflective Questions:

1. Why is it essential to understand that gender and chromosomes don't always align neatly into male or female?
2. How do the stories of those with chromosomal variations challenge our traditional understanding of gender?
3. In what ways does society's emphasis on binary gender impact individuals with non-traditional chromosomal structures?
4. How can you cultivate empathy and understanding for those whose chromosomal or genital presentation might differ from societal expectations?

Family Exercise: Chromosome Art Activity

Materials:
- Drawing paper
- Colored pencils, crayons, or markers
- Printed or digital images of chromosomes (for reference)

Instructions:

1. Introduction to Chromosomes: Begin by explaining that every person has chromosomes that provide the blueprint for our bodies. Mention the usual pairs, XX for females and XY for males, but emphasize that nature has variations.
2. Drawing Activity: Invite each family member to draw what they believe XX, XY, XXY, XO, and XXX chromosomes might look like, using the reference images to help guide them.
3. Discussion: After drawing, discuss the different types of chromosomes and the physical manifestations they might produce. Address any misconceptions or questions that arise.
4. Empathy Building: Share the stories of children with various chromosomal configurations, emphasizing their lived experiences over medical details. Discuss how society might treat these individuals and how they can foster a more understanding and inclusive environment.
5. Wrap-up: End the activity by asking family members to share one thing they've learned or one way their perspective has shifted.

This exercise aims to foster understanding and empathy by combining hands-on learning with reflective conversation, highlighting the beauty of human diversity.

CHAPTER 8: ANSWERING THE QUESTION: WHY DO PEOPLE TRANSITION?

Our quest for self-identity is as natural as breathing. Our history, vibrancy, colors, rhythms, and stories shared throughout time stand tall as a universal pilgrimage. Following one's call to live their truth is the journey's driving force. For some, this journey involves transitioning - a transformative experience that speaks of deep spiritual attunement, ancestral echoes, and the yearning for existential harmony. What does this this sacred exploration entail?

The Spiritual Call of Authenticity

The Earth has borne witness to wide-reaching souls and stories, each navigating their divine paths, echoing the universe's vibrancy. Just as every stream seeks the ocean, every heart seeks its authentic rhythm. Transitioning for many is akin to a river's destined journey to the ocean, heeding the soul's call and aligning with its spiritual compass.

Empathic spirituality, with its beautiful traditions and deep connections to nature, teaches that life is a wonderful synthesis of both seen and unseen forces. Transitioning can be likened to the dance of the African Masai, filled with vitality and meaning, a dance that celebrates the soul's whisper and passion.

Ancestral Timbres

The historical blend of our many cultures and their descendants provides a window into the wisdom of our ancestors. As we learned in our brief look through history, many communities understood and valued individuals who transcended societal gender norms.

Drawing strength from this wisdom, one can recognize that transitioning is not merely a modern pursuit but a timeless spiritual manifestation. It's an affirmation that the essence of gender, surpassing limitations established by the rules of men, is a sacred energy echoing through time.

Harmonizing Inner and Outer Kingdoms

Everything in existence seeks balance. This principle, fundamental to energetic cosmology, also finds familiarity in the transgender experience. When an individual's inner self does not align with the societal reflections they encounter, a spiritual discord ensues. They begin to energetically attune to their ideal self and thus begin to attract those people, situations, and reality that aligns with their emitted frequency. Transitioning then becomes an act of restoration and balance, a harmonization of the inner melody with the external world's rhythm.

Prevailing Affirmation and Celebrating Truth

Beyond physical and emotional chasms lie the domain of existential truth. Every soul yearns for this validation - a universal affirmation of existence. For many transgender individuals, transitioning is this universe's echo, a powerful "I see you in your entirety."

The world's affirmation, while nurturing, is secondary. The primary celebration emerges from within, where the soul acknowledges its radiant truth.

Exploring Deeper: A Personal Journey

My personal journey has been both insightful and transformative; no pun intended. I've danced with my shadows (i.e. shadow work), embraced the light, and found harmony amidst chaos. My spiritual team's whispers guided me, and the wisdom of my connected intuition lit my path.

Transitioning was not just about aligning with my true gender identity but also about reclaiming my space in the sacred circle of life. It was about honoring the divine within Me and recognizing that my existence, like that of countless others, added a brilliant note to the universe's song.

Reflective Questions:

1. Can you recall moments when you felt a deep yearning to reflect your inner truths outwardly?
2. How does the concept of balance manifest in your personal experiences?
3. Drawing from our shared ancestral wisdom, can you identify other instances in history or cultures where individuals transcended societal expectations?

Family Exercise: The Web of Authenticity

Objective: To interconnect and celebrate each family member's true essence, weaving a shared symbol of authenticity.

Instructions:

1. Sit together in a circle, each holding a ball of yarn or string.
2. Begin by stating one authentic truth about yourself and then pass the ball of yarn to another family member while holding onto the end of the string.
3. As each member shares their truth, they hold a part of the string and pass the ball to the next person.
4. Eventually, a web forms, symbolizing the interconnectedness of each individual's authentic truth.

Traversing this journey offers an in-depth understanding and respect for the reasons individuals transition. The path is not just of personal transformation but of the timeless dance of souls seeking their divine counterparts in the vast cosmos.

CHAPTER 9: ANSWERING THE QUESTION: WHY DO PEOPLE DETRANSITION?

We wholly accept that identity is fluid, ever-shifting. For some, transitioning is justly the most authentic step toward alignment with their true self. For others, the journey continues beyond transition, leading them toward a different path, one of detransition. Detransitioning is not a failure, nor does it erase the truth of the experiences that came before it. It is another step in a deeply personal, spiritual, and energetic process of becoming.

Many who detransition still identify as part of the LGBTQIA2S+ family, holding space in the beautiful community of all that is humanity. This journey, like all journeys of self-discovery, requires deep reflection, self-compassion, and the unwavering support of those who love them

Through discussions with those who have decided to alter their path, the reasons behind detransitioning are diverse and highly individualized; reinforcing that gender identity is not static, but an unfolding process of self-realization[37].

What Does It Mean to Detransition?

For some, detransitioning means returning to a gender identity that aligns with their gender assigned at birth, but for many others, it is about realizing that gender exists in fluidity, not finality. Some who detransition find that

---

[37] Littman L. Individuals Treated for Gender Dysphoria with Medical and/or Surgical Transition Who Subsequently Detransitioned: A Survey of 100 Detransitioners. Arch Sex Behav. 2021;50(8):3353-3369. doi:10.1007/s10508-021-02163-w

they are intersex, or that they feel most at home in a non-binary identity, existing outside of traditional categories. Regardless of the direction, detransitioning is not a reversal, it is an expansion of understanding.

Like all aspects of personal growth, transitioning and detransitioning are deeply spiritual and energetic processes. They are acts of alignment, of seeking wholeness, of listening to the internal voice that whispers, "This is who I am". No one else can dictate that truth, and no one should shame another for walking a path that leads them to greater clarity. To detransition is to explore what feels most authentic in the present moment, recognizing that identity is a process, not a destination.

Why Would Someone Choose to Detransition?

There are many reasons why someone may choose to detransition, and each story is unique. Some individuals realize that a medical transition was not necessary for them to affirm their identity. Others detransition due to external pressures, such as a lack of familial support, societal discrimination, or barriers to accessing affirming healthcare. For some, transitioning may have provided a temporary sense of relief, but as they evolved, they'd come to understand their gender in a different way.

Medical or psychological concerns can also be factors. Some individuals experience complications from hormone therapy or surgery that make them reconsider their transition path. Others may struggle with co-existing mental health conditions that complicate their sense of identity.

We have come to understand that the percentage of transgender individuals in the United States who have gone through detransition is relatively small. Though the number is low, it is still important to understand. Published in the journal LGBT Health by Turban et al. analyzed data from the U.S. Transgender Survey (USTS), which included over 27,000 respondents[38]. Of this study, only 13.1% or 3,150 transgender individuals reported having ever detransitioned at some point in their lives. This means that many of the 13.1% has continued their transition journey.

Sixty-two percent or 1,953 of those who detransitioned did so only temporarily; often due to external pressures such as family rejection, lack of support, or financial barriers, not because they no longer identified as transgender. Subsequently, they are still trans-identified.

---

[38] Turban, J. L., King, D., Carswell, J. M., & Keuroghlian, A. S. (2021). Detransition Among Transgender and Gender Diverse People: A Survey of US Adults. LGBT Health, 8(4), 273–280. https://doi.org/10.1089/lgbt.2020.0483

Only about 2.4% or 648 of the total 27,000 respondents permanently detransitioned and no longer identified as transgender at the time of the survey. This data reinforces that while detransition is a real and valid part of some people's journeys, the overwhelming majority of transgender people do not regret transitioning and do not choose to detransition. It's important to approach this subject with compassion.

Another in-depth study of 100 individuals who detransitioned was published in Archives of Sexual Behavior. It found that the reasons for detransitioning varied widely, with participants confirming personal, medical, social, and psychological factors[39]. Thirty-eight percent of the study participants shared that they had arrived at the conclusion that their original desire to transition was caused by trauma and abuse. Fifty-five percent felt they had not receive sufficient care from a physician or psychiatrist before beginning their transition. Some had begun the process on their own without medical guidance. Under the care of a mental health professional, one is more likely to be guided down the path that best aligns with their ideal self. This reminds us that gender is not one-size-fits-all and that self-discovery is a deeply personal process.

The Potential Negatives of Detransitioning

For Our Young Ones
When our children begin to explore their gender identity, they require support, patience, and access to affirming care. Detransitioning for our young ones usually involves only changing their names again, a different wardrobe, or hair style. If a child chooses to detransition, they may feel guilt or fear that they have "disappointed" their family or community. They may also struggle with a renewed sense of dysphoria or confusion, particularly if they detransition due to external pressure rather than personal choice. If the guardian in their life respond with shame or dismissal, our young ones may internalize feelings of self-doubt, leading to anxiety or depression.

For The Mature Beings
For adults, detransitioning can bring slightly different challenges. They may experience a loss of community, as even those within the LGBTQIA2S+ community may not fully understand or support detransitioned individuals. As adults are more likely to have had begun hormone therapy or completed as least one surgical procedure, they may struggle with medical complications;

---

[39] Littman L. Individuals Treated for Gender Dysphoria with Medical and/or Surgical Transition Who Subsequently Detransitioned: A Survey of 100 Detransitioners. Arch Sex Behav. 2021;50(8):3353-3369. doi:10.1007/s10508-021-02163-w

requiring additional healthcare interventions. There is also the reality of facing external judgment. Some individuals may use detransitioning as "proof" that being transgender is not real, which can be deeply harmful to the soul walking a new path and the transgender community as a whole. The psychological effects of detransitioning can be complex, requiring support and guidance from affirming professionals and loved ones.

The Potential Positives of Detransitioning

For Our Young Ones
Children who detransition after exploring their gender identity may experience relief in discovering a clearer sense of self. Rather than seeing it as a mistake, it can be a powerful learning experience that helps them better understand their relationship with gender. Parents and caregivers should view detransitioning not as an endpoint, but as part of the child's journey toward self-awareness. When handled with love and openness, children can grow into confident, self-assured individuals who feel safe exploring who they are.

For The Mature Beings
For adults, detransitioning can be liberating if it is done as part of their journey toward authenticity. Some find that detransitioning allows them to embrace aspects of their identity they had not previously considered, such as realizing they are intersex or non-binary. Others find peace in returning to a place that feels more natural for them. The most positive aspect of detransitioning is the ability to fully embrace one's truth; a truth without shame, without apology, and without external pressures dictating the course of their identity.

Support Needed From Their Family, Friends, and The Community

Someone considering detransitioning needs what all people need, love, understanding, and patience. They need to know that their worth is not tied to how others perceive their gender but to the truth they hold within. Supporters should create an open, non-judgmental space for them to process their feelings, ask questions, and express their fears.

It is crucial to remember that detransitioning does not mean they have made a mistake, nor is it a betrayal of the transgender or LGBTQIA2S+ community. It is simply another step in the individual's journey of self-discovery. Those who are supportive can validate their loved one's experience by affirming that identity is personal and that there is no shame in changing course.

The Defense Of The Detransitioner

The decision to detransition often invites scrutiny from those who do not understand the fluidity of gender and identity. Ignorant, poorly educated, and hateful individuals may question their choices or use their journey to discredit the transgender experience as a whole. It is important to stand firm in one's truth.

One way to defend one's path is through education. Sharing the reality that gender exploration is a natural part of maturity and that detransitioning does not invalidate anyone's lived experience. Those who detransition can also set boundaries with those who seek to undermine them, choosing to engage only in conversations that come from a place of genuine curiosity and respect. You are not required to remain in spaces where you are not respected. Allow your boundaries to be your words, you room, your home, or a protective organization.

Above all, those who detransition must prioritize their own well-being. The universe does not require justification for change. Just as the stars shift their positions over time, just as the tides ebb and flow, so too does human identity move in the direction of alignment. No one else can dictate what is right for your soul. Every journey, whether toward transition, detransition, or a place in between, is sacred and deserving of respect.

For those who choose this path, the most vital thing is not the labels they leave behind or the ones they adopt, but the peace they find in living as their most authentic self. The greatest gift we can offer those on this journey, whether transitioning, detransitioning, or simply existing, is the assurance that they are seen, they are valued, and they are never alone.

Reflective Questions:

1. What does it mean to explore who you are, and why do you think people sometimes change how they express themselves?
2. How would you feel if someone told you that you weren't allowed to be yourself? How do you think we can support someone who is figuring out who they are?
3. Why do you think it's important to listen to people's stories without judgment, even if their journey is different from our own?

Family Exercise: The Web of Authenticity

<u>Objective:</u> To help children understand that everyone's journey to self-

discovery is unique and that changes in identity, like detransitioning, are part of growing and learning. This activity will encourage empathy, curiosity, and support for people as they navigate who they are.

Materials:
- A large piece of paper or poster board
- Colored markers, crayons, or stickers
- Small cut-out paper stars or sticky notes

Instructions:

1. Create the Pathway: Draw a long, winding road on the paper. At different points along the road, draw stops, rest areas, or symbols that represent moments of change or self-discovery.
2. Adding the Stars: Give each family member several small paper stars or sticky notes. Ask them to write down different moments in their life when they learned something new about themselves (for example: discovering a new hobby, making a new friend, or changing their mind about something important).
3. Connecting to the Lesson: As everyone adds their stars to the pathway, discuss how learning about yourself is something that happens over time. Some people may go in one direction for a while and then realize they need to take another path. That is truly a personal choice. People change, grow, and discover what feels right for them.
4. Talk About Support: Ask the family, "What can we do when someone in our family or community is trying to figure out who they are? How can we help them feel safe and loved?" Encourage children to think about small acts of kindness, like listening without judgment, using someone's chosen name, or standing up for a friend
5. Final Reflection: End the activity by reminding everyone that everyone's path is different, and just like the stars in the night sky, each journey is valid, beautiful, and uniquely important.

Our multiverse never stops shifting, neither does the evolution of the Self. Detransitioning is not an ending, it is a continuation of the path toward wholeness. Whether one transitions, detransitions, or moves between expressions of gender fluidity, the core truth remains: they are worthy of love, respect, and self-acceptance.

CHAPTER 10: DEBUNKING MYTHS: CLEARING UP LIES & COMMON MISUNDERSTANDINGS

It's essential to clear the mists of misconceptions that often cloud our vision. Walking this path, we uncover truths, layer by layer, dispelling myths and bridging gaps of misunderstanding. As I have personally discussed these myths with others to elevate them from a place of understanding, I'm honored to guide you through this illuminating process, reaffirming the importance of embracing our shared humanity.

Myth 1: Being Transgender Is a Choice

For many, the heart knows its truth even before words can define it. Being transgender isn't a whimsical decision or a chosen path; it's a deeply-rooted understanding of oneself, an alignment of one's soul and identity. Just as the sun doesn't choose to rise or the river to flow, a transgender individual doesn't choose their identity—it simply is.

Myth 2: Transgender People Are "Confused"

Confusion is a state of not understanding, a mix of unclear intentions. But for many transgender individuals, their clarity about their identity is unwavering. It is society's preconceived notions and biases that often label this clarity as "confusion." Let's replace misunderstanding with empathy, realizing that each person's journey to self-discovery is remarkable and sacred. The process of identifying one's truth involves many discussions with ourselves, mental health professionals, medical professionals, holistic practitioners, guardians and parents, counselors, friends, and family members. Having access to freely engage in these intense investigations with the assistance of our supporters lays the foundations for developing a string sense of self with the utmost clarity. This is why transgender health care for children is extremely important. With each declaration and discovery, transgender and non-binary people grow to become the most self-aware and socially informed human beings within this known multi-verse. They learn how to navigate the subtle and dangerous nuances of existence. With the community behind us, we don't just survive, we thrive!

Myth 3: All Transgender People Undergo Medical Transition

The journey of every transgender person is distinctive. While some may seek medical interventions to align their physical selves with their gender identity, others might not. Neither journey is more valid than the other. Consider the transgender and non-binary population of our ancient cultures. The concept of medical transition was not widely understood, let alone being practiced. It's essential to recognize and respect individual choices, understanding that there's no one "right" way to be transgender.

Myth 4: Gender Identity and Sexual Orientation Are the Same

Gender identity revolves around one's internal understanding of being male, female, both, or neither. In contrast, sexual orientation pertains to whom one is attracted to emotionally, romantically, or physically. They are distinct aspects of one's identity, and it's crucial to differentiate between the two, granting each its due importance.

Myth 5: Children Are Too Young to Know Their Gender Identity

It is a common misconception that children are too young to understand their own gender identity. However, research in developmental psychology and pediatrics shows that many children become aware of and begin to express their gender identity between the ages of two and four[40][41]. Childhood is a time of exploration and self-discovery. Children have an innate sense of self that often shines through their words, actions, and preferences, even before they can fully articulate it Just as children have an intimate

---

[40] American Psychological Association. (2015). Guidelines for psychological practice with transgender and gender nonconforming people. American Psychologist, 70(9), 832–864. https://doi.org/10.1037/a0039906

[41] Rafferty, J., AAP Committee on Psychosocial Aspects of Child and Family Health, AAP Committee on Adolescence, & Section on Lesbian, Gay, Bisexual, and Transgender Health and Wellness. (2018). Ensuring comprehensive care and support for transgender and gender-diverse children and adolescents. Pediatrics, 142(4), e20182162. https://doi.org/10.1542/peds.2018-2162

understanding of their likes and dislikes, dreams, and fears, they can also possess a deeply-rooted awareness of their gender identity. It is not about rushing them into any particular identity or choice, but rather acknowledging their experiences, listening to their voices, and providing them with the love, guidance, and support they need to grow into their authentic selves. It's vital to provide them with a safe space, allowing them to express and understand themselves freely.

It may help to remember that a child's developing sense of identity is influenced by biological, emotional, and social factors. When parents, guardians, and caregivers validate and respect a young person's expressions of gender, research suggests it can lead to better mental health outcomes and decreased anxiety or depression later in life[42]. The image of self in this multiverse begins to hold deeper meaning. Conversely, denying or suppressing our young one's identity can create confusion and distress, potentially complicating their emotional development. By offering understanding, acceptance, and guidance, we empower our children to explore and affirm who they are from a place of safety and respect, rather than fear or judgment.

Myth 6: Being Transgender is a New Phenomenon

It's easy to think that the conversation about being transgender is modern because it's more visible in today's media versus being widely taught in school. However, transgender and gender non-conforming individuals have existed in various cultures worldwide for centuries. From the two-spirit people of Indigenous cultures in North America to India's Hijras and the sister girls and brother boys of the Indigenous Australians, gender diversity has been acknowledged and respected in various forms. Due to the discrimination and demonization imposed following Christian colonization, transgender and non-binary individuals learned how to survive from the shadows. However, as more humans began to educate themselves on the history and cultures of which transgender people existed, they became more open and accepting. This inclusive disposition helped to encourage more transgender people to live their truth, and in many instances, demand their universally given right to be treated equally.

Myth 7: Transgender People Are Just Seeking Attention

Such a perspective reduces the delicate journey of identity and self-

---

[42] Olson, K. R., Durwood, L., DeMeules, M., & McLaughlin, K. A. (2016). Mental health of transgender children who are supported in their identities. Pediatrics, 137(3), e20153223. https://doi.org/10.1542/peds.2015-3223

recognition that transgender individuals go through to mere theatrics. In reality, many transgender individuals fear negative attention and discrimination. If transgender people were not discriminated against, abused, and silenced, then there would be no need to "fight" back. If transgender people were treated respectfully as human beings, there would be no need for PRIDE (which essentially began as a protest to the inhumane and out right criminal treatment of those of the LGBT community). Their journey is about authenticity, not attention.

Myth 8: Transgender Individuals are Deceptive

There's a harmful stereotype that transgender people are trying to "trick" or "deceive" others about their "real" gender. This misconception can be dangerous, leading to discrimination or even violence. Being authentic to one's self isn't deception; it's an act of courage and truth.

Myth 9: It's Just a Phase

This myth invalidates and trivializes the lived experiences of transgender individuals. Like everyone else, transgender individuals have an in-depth understanding of themselves. Dismissing their identity as a "phase" is an oversimplification of their delicate journey to self-realization.

Myth 10: Transgender People Are Trying to Force Your Children to Transition

Walking this path you must acknowledge that no one can truly force another's journey. Each soul chooses its own path and seeks its own truth. Transgender individuals only ask for acceptance and understanding for their personal choices, just as we all do. The notion that they might influence or force someone else, especially a child, to transition is an unfounded fear. The essence of any spiritual teaching is respect for each individual's journey, and the same holds true for the transgender and non-binary community. Forcing a child to make such a change lays the foundation for an adult who resents not only themselves, but all who were involved in their life's transition. This does not positively serve the transgender community in any way, form, nor fashion.

Myth 11: Doctors Are Forcing Toddlers and Children to Undergo Genital Surgery

When it comes to the care and well-being of young individuals, medical decisions, especially as life-altering as gender confirmation surgery, are approached with careful reflection and the utmost care. The World Professional Association for Transgender Health (WPATH), a leading international, interdisciplinary professional organization, has established clear standards of care to ensure that transgender and gender non-conforming people receive safe and effective medical care.

According to WPATH's Standards of Care (Version 7)[43], several requirements must be fulfilled before a person under the age of 18 receives a recommendation for gender confirmation surgery:

> 1. Persistent, well-documented gender dysphoria: This involves a comprehensive assessment to ensure that the individual's feelings and experiences are consistent and deeply rooted.
>
> 2. Capacity to give informed consent: While this is typically expected of adults, minors must have the capacity to fully understand the potential risks, benefits, and consequences of the procedure.
>
> 3. Age of majority in a given country: If they haven't reached the age of majority, which varies by country, surgery should be approached with added caution, involving consent from the parents or guardians.
>
> 4. Significant medical and mental health care: Individuals must undergo a period of continuous hormone therapy appropriate to the patient's gender goals unless hormones are not clinically indicated for the individual. Moreover, if significant medical or mental health concerns are present, they must be reasonably well-controlled.
>
> 5. Consistent and lived gender role: WPATH emphasizes the importance of the individual living in a gender role that is congruent with their gender identity for a significant period before surgery.

Understanding these guidelines, it's clear that the pathway to surgery is neither impulsive nor forced. It's a weighty and thoughtful journey, informed by medical expertise, ethical considerations, and the individual's personal desires, needs, and experiences.

Published in 2022, the groundbreaking study "Prevalence of Gender-Affirming Surgical Procedures Among Minors and Adults in the United States" by Roberts and colleagues in JAMA provides crucial clarity about the

---

[43] World Professional Association for Transgender Health, "Standards of Care for the Health of Transsexual, Transgender, and Gender Nonconforming People," Version 7

realities of gender-affirming care. Contrary to misconceptions, the study found that no gender-affirming surgeries were performed on transgender minors under the age of 12. Among minors aged 12 and older, such surgeries were exceedingly rare, with almost all procedures involving chest-related surgeries for adolescents aged 15 to 17. According to the William Institute of UCLA's School of Law, approximately 300,000 individuals under the age of 17 identify as transgender in the United States[44]. I must reiterate that trans-identified children under the age of twelve were not having surgical procedures to affirm their gender. These findings emphasize that fears surrounding widespread surgeries on young transgender individuals are unfounded and are often rooted in misinformation.

The JAMA study also highlights an essential but frequently overlooked fact: gender-affirming surgeries are not exclusive to transgender individuals. Cisgender people, too, undergo procedures that align with their gender identities. For example, cisgender men who experience gynecomastia, a condition causing breast tissue growth, may receive breast reduction surgery as a form of gender-affirming care. In fact, the study revealed that the majority of breast reduction surgeries in the dataset were performed on cisgender men rather than transgender individuals. This nuance underscores the importance of understanding gender-affirming care as a broad and inclusive concept, benefiting people across all gender identities.

What's particularly revealing in this discussion is how conservative activists often conflate data about intersex and transgender surgeries to paint a distorted picture. These groups frequently cite procedures performed on intersex infants, often without consent, as part of their narrative against transgender care for minors. In reality, such intersex-related surgeries are a separate ethical issue and not reflective of transgender healthcare practices, which adhere to stringent standards of care. As this study demonstrates, decisions about gender-affirming surgeries for transgender minors are deliberate, heavily regulated, and guided by evidence-based protocols

As a spiritual healer, I see this conversation as an opportunity to shift from fear-driven narratives to compassion and understanding. The truth, backed by research, is that transgender and non-binary individuals seek gender-affirming care to align their physical selves with their fundamental, energetic, and even spiritual truths. The path to healing is not one-size-fits-all, and for minors, this journey is approached with great care, collaboration between families and professionals, and a commitment to the well-being of

---

[44] Williams Institute. June 2022. "How Many Adults and Youth Identify as Transgender in the United States?" UCLA School of Law. https://williamsinstitute.law.ucla.edu/publications/trans-adults-united-states/

the individual.

The spirit's call for alignment and authenticity is sacred, and the medical community, guided by entities like WPATH, and supported by truth explorers like UCLA and JAMA seeks to honor that call with respect, care, and wisdom. Let us honor this truth with respect and empathy, leaving no room for myths or misinformation to sow doubt in the hearts of those seeking peace in their authentic selves.

Myth 12: Transgender People Are Possessed By Evil Spirits or the Devil

Throughout history, things not immediately understood were often labeled as the work of malevolent spirits. In 2024, to my face, my father told me that I was not only being seduced, but also possessed by the devil. Viewing from a more piratical sense, a Christian believes the Devil is an evil Being full of negativity who destroys and tears at the souls of others. In this interaction, we can clearly see who was destructive, full of negativity and sought to harm the soul of another.

Before you take it upon yourself to label another individual as evil or under the influence of negativity, you should first assess your heart, your mind, and your motives behind your words and actions. As a spiritual seeker, I personally believe in the inherent divinity of every soul, understanding that each individual is a magnificent expression of the universal energy. To say transgender individuals are possessed is to misunderstand the divine spectrum of human experience. Every heart beats to the resonance of the same cosmic rhythm; every soul carries a spark of the sacred flame.

Myth 13: Men Want to Identify As Women Only To Enter the Women's Restroom

Dignity and authenticity guide a person's journey to embrace their true gender identity. It's a deep and often challenging voyage, motivated by an innate desire to align one's external world with their internal truth. The notion that someone would undergo the complexities of transitioning simply to access a particular restroom diminishes the complex nature of this journey. It's as if they believe the "dreaded" women's bathroom sign is a protective talisman that thwarts an abuser from entering the women's lavatory. Trust that every soul seeks its truth for reasons far deeper and more sacred than the physical spaces they occupy.

In our quest for knowledge, let us be guided by compassion and understanding, looking beyond myths to see the radiant souls that reside within us all.

The Path to Understanding

The illumination that comes from dispelling myths is far-reaching. As these misconceptions fade away, we pave the path for acceptance, compassion, and unity. This journey isn't just about understanding the transgender community - it's about deepening our understanding of humanity.

We realize that the spiritual teaching in Earth realm show that our true essence lies beyond labels, beyond myths, and beyond biases. Our spirits resonate with the energies of the universe, transcending societal constructs. By debunking these myths, we don't just foster an environment of acceptance for the transgender community, we nurture a world where every soul, regardless of gender identity, finds its rightful place. The journey may be long, but with every myth debunked, we light a torch of truth that brightens the path ahead.

Reflective Questions:

1. How have the debunking of these myths challenged or reshaped your previous understanding?
2. Why do you think society clings to certain misconceptions about the transgender community?
3. How can awareness and education serve as tools to dispel myths in your community?

Family Exercise: The Tree of Truths

Objective: This activity aims to help families visualize the process of debunking myths, using the metaphor of a tree to "shed" misconceptions and "grow" truths.

Instructions:

1. Draw a large tree on a piece of paper or cardboard. Label it "The Tree of Truths."
2. Write down common myths about transgender individuals on leaves. Attach these leaves to the tree's branches.
3. As you discuss each myth and its debunking as a family, remove the corresponding leaf and replace it with a fruit labeled with the truth or understanding that dispels the myth.

4. Encourage open dialogue. Allow family members, especially children, to ask questions, express feelings, or share insights.
5. Once all the myths have been replaced with truths, reflect on the tree's transformation, symbolizing the family's evolving understanding.

Every tree, every leaf, and every fruit tells a story. As we nurture our Tree of Truths, we are reminded of the ever-evolving nature of understanding, the shedding of biases, and the blossoming of acceptance. Let's cherish this growth, for in doing so, we celebrate the limitless beauty of human diversity.

CHAPTER 11: EMBRACING EVERYONE: THE IMPORTANCE OF ACCEPTANCE

Stare with me, if you will, into the night's sky. The trillion-piece puzzle of the Milky Way holds representations of each of us as a singular and irreplaceable piece. We come in various shades, shapes, and narratives, each contributing to the breathtaking beauty of the Whole. I've found myself standing at the vantage point from where the entire masterpiece is visible, and I'm consistently awe-inspired by its splendor and intricacy. Yet, the magnificence is not just in the collective; it's in every single piece, in every individual's story.

A Personal Odyssey

My personal journey towards self-discovery and authenticity was similar to navigating a labyrinth. Paths converged, diverged, and occasionally led to places of deep introspection. Many times, the surroundings seemed shadowy, filled with societal misunderstandings and prejudices. However, the eternal spirit within, which knows no boundaries of religion nor societal constructs, continually guided me towards truth, love, and enlightenment.

The beauty of this journey, as many of you might resonate with, is in its universality and yet its distinctive nature. Just as no two pieces in a mosaic design are the same, every individual's journey to self-acceptance and realization is different. Recognizing and honoring this diversity is the essence of true acceptance.

Beyond Tolerance: The Heart of Genuine Acceptance

To many, acceptance might be synonymous with tolerance. But in the factual sense, there's a chasm between the two. Tolerance is passive - it's merely an act of endurance. Acceptance, on the other hand, is active, vibrant, and life-affirming. It's about embracing others with all your heart, seeing them for who they truly are, and celebrating their essence.

At the core of acceptance is a comprehensive realization: every being is an expression of the same cosmic energy. We may don diverse attires, adopt varied roles, and even express contrasting beliefs, but at our essence, we are interconnected by the same life force. This truth forms the crux of my teachings. When you truly understand and internalize this concept, acceptance is no longer a chore; it's a natural expression of your being.

The transformative power of acceptance is also palpable in its ability to heal wounds, bridge divides, and foster communities. Accepting someone is akin to recognizing the divine within them. You recognize the sacred energy within them. This not only empowers the individual but also elevates the collective consciousness of the community.

On my journey, acceptance was never limited to my personal transgender experience. It extended far beyond, into realms of embracing every shade of human experience. Each story, each challenge, each victory, and even each setback carries a lesson, a message. Embracing all these narratives enhances our understanding of life and strengthens our spiritual perspective.

The Ripple Effects of Acceptance

Acceptance has a transformative power. It not only impacts the individual who is being accepted but also creates ripples in families, communities, and societies. When one person chooses to live authentically in love and positivity and is embraced for it, it inspires others to do the same. It sends a message that their individuality and truth is valued, that diversity is celebrated, and that love transcends biases and misconceptions.

I've experienced this transformative power firsthand. Acceptance has not just been about my trans-identity, but it has also been about embracing others in all their beautiful diversity, realizing that our collective strength lies in our remarkable stories and experiences.

Reflection and Transformation

By contemplating on these insights, it becomes evident that acceptance is more than a mere concept - it's a way of life, a transformative tool. And if we're to create a future where every individual feels cherished and valued, we must begin by instilling these values in the very heart of our families.

Reflective Questions:

1. In your own words, how would you differentiate between tolerance and acceptance?
2. Recall a personal experience where you felt deeply accepted. How did that shape your sense of self-worth?
3. In what ways can you foster an environment of genuine acceptance within your immediate community?

Family Exercise: The Tree of Embrace

Objective: This activity aims to instill the values of acceptance within families, allowing each member to understand the beauty of individuality and the strength of collective embrace.

Instructions:

1. Gather as a family and create a 'Tree' on a large piece of paper.
2. Each family member gets a leaf on which they write something they genuinely appreciate about themselves and another family member.
3. Attach these leaves to the Tree.
4. Engage in a discussion about the feelings that emerged from this activity. Delve deep into topics of self-acceptance, embracing diversity, and the joys of collective love.

The 'Tree of Embrace' stands as a symbol of growth, unity, and collective strength. It's a reminder that every person, with their individuality, contributes to the overall well-being and growth of the family.

As we journey forward, let's remember the transformative power of acceptance. By embracing everyone in their authentic essence, we are not just nurturing individuals; we are elevating the collective spirit of humanity. Together, let's weave a world filled with understanding, compassion, and universal love.

CHAPTER 12: RECOGNIZING FEELINGS: EMPATHY AND THE TRANSGENDER EXPERIENCE

Life is a song of emotions, patterns of frequencies, where each tone represents a different feeling. From joy's exuberant highs to sorrow's melancholic lows, our lives waltz to this mesmerizing music, which is full, ever changing, and deeply evocative. This journey has taught me that while our individual melodies may differ, the essence of what we feel is universally human.

The Landscape of Empathy

Empathy is more than just feeling sympathy for someone; it's about understanding and sharing the emotions another person is experiencing. The ability to deeply resonate with another's feelings is an innate human trait. Yet, in our diverse world, the challenge is often to bridge the gap between different life experiences and understand feelings that might be far from our own lived realities.

For many transgender individuals, our journey is one of deep introspection, courage, and authenticity. The path to understanding and embracing our true selves can be arduous, filled with challenges, but also moments of pure glee and happiness. Sharing this journey with others, helping them feel even a fraction of our experiences, is where empathy plays a key role.

A Transgender Perspective

Imagine waking up each day feeling like your reflection belongs to someone else. It's not just about the physical features that don't align with your soul, it's the disconnect, the feeling of not being seen for who you truly are. For me, being transgender has been a journey of uncovering, layer by layer, the essence of who I've always been. It's not a path I chose, but a truth I had to honor, despite the many hurdles placed in my way.

The world often asks transgender individuals to explain themselves, to justify their existence, their decisions, their authenticity. But imagine if, instead of interrogating, people simply paused to listen. If they saw us as human beings navigating an often-hostile world while seeking only to live as our most authentic selves. When I share my story, I'm not just asking for acceptance; I'm offering a piece of my truth in the hopes that it resonates, that it stirs compassion. Being transgender isn't about rejecting who I was, it's about embracing who I've always been, even in the face of societal misunderstanding.

This journey isn't just about transition; it's about healing. It's about bridging the gap between the inner self and the outer world, finding a sense of alignment that allows me to exist in harmony. Every step, every struggle, every triumph has taught me the value of empathy, not just from others but also for myself. Being transgender has taught me that our greatest strength lies in our ability to feel deeply, to love expansively, and to see beyond labels. In sharing this perspective, my hope is to open hearts to the truth that our differences are not divisions but bridges to a deeper understanding of one another.

By bridging connections with our essence, we see that our struggles and joys, while differing in their narrative, resonate with universal emotions. Feelings of longing, love, acceptance, fear, courage, and hope are universal. By recognizing these shared emotional frequencies, we foster a genuine understanding and empathy towards the transgender community.

The Importance of Recognizing Feelings

For parents, guardians, and care givers, fostering a space where feelings are recognized, understood, and validated is crucial. When children see emotions as something natural and acceptable to discuss, it opens doors for meaningful conversations about diverse experiences, including the transgender journey. It's not merely about explaining a concept but letting them feel the emotions tied to it.

The spiritual teachings I've embraced emphasize that at our core, beyond the layers of identity, emotions, and experiences, we are beings of pure energy and love. By tapping into this universal love, we transcend biases and prejudices, reaching a space of genuine understanding and empathy.

Reflective Questions:

1. Can you recall a time when you felt deeply empathetic towards someone whose experiences were vastly different from yours? What triggered this empathy?
2. How do you perceive the balance between understanding the particular challenges of the transgender community and recognizing the universal emotions they feel?
3. How can embracing one's spiritual essence pave the way for deeper empathy and understanding?

Family Exercise: Emotional Storytelling

Objective: To foster a deeper understanding of diverse emotions and experiences.

Instructions:

1. Sit together as a family. Each member shares a story or an experience from their day, emphasizing the emotions they felt.
2. After each story, the other members share how the story made them feel and if they can relate to those feelings.
3. Finally, discuss the similarities in the emotions everyone felt, regardless of the different experiences.

This exercise not only brings families closer but also emphasizes the universality of emotions. It serves as a gentle reminder that no matter how diverse our experiences, our feelings connect us in significant and meaningful ways.

The journey to understanding and empathy is continuous and ever-evolving. Recognizing feelings, both our own and those of others, is the bridge that connects diverse lives and narratives. Through empathy, we don't just understand the transgender experience; we embrace the universal human journey of emotions, growth, and intense spiritual realization.

CHAPTER 13: ADDRESSING BULLYING: STANDING UP FOR WHAT'S RIGHT

A picture is worth more than a thousand words. Take a snap shot of your life today. Stare at it. Every part represents a story, a journey, and a lesson. My narrative is a testament to resilience, understanding, and the unyielding spirit of human connection. Among the many experiences I've encountered, bullying holds a substantial place. While its darkness is undeniable, there's also a potential for insightful transformation, learning, and growth.

The Spectrum of Understanding

> Recognizing the Unknown:
> Bullying is, in essence, rooted in the unknown. Things or Beings that are different or unfamiliar often become targets. But with this very unfamiliarity lies our greatest strength - the power to educate, to enlighten, and to foster acceptance.
>
> Transcending Fear:
> The unknown often leads to fear, which can manifest as prejudice, hatred, and even bullying. By understanding the root of such fears and addressing them with love and knowledge, we can pave the way for more compassionate interactions.

Roots of Bullying

> Diving Deep:
> Bullying is not a superficial problem. Its roots can often be traced to

feelings of inadequacy, personal traumas, societal pressures, or misunderstandings. Understanding this can shift our perspective from pure resentment to empathy, not for the act but for the individual and their struggles.

Breaking the Cycle:
Recognizing the root causes of bullying helps in breaking the vicious cycle. By offering support, understanding, and therapeutic interventions to bullies, we can potentially prevent further instances and begin healing the larger community.

From Darkness to Light

Choosing Compassion over Confrontation:
As a spiritual guide, I've realized that our reactions mold our realities. Reacting with compassion and an intent to educate rather than confront can transform potential conflicts into moments of growth and illumination.

Shifting Narratives:
When faced with negativity, we have the choice to either feed it or redirect it. Sharing personal stories, offering insights, and creating dialogues can shift the narrative from misunderstanding to mutual respect.

Empowerment through Knowledge

Storytelling as a Tool:
Each of our stories is a lesson waiting to be shared. By actively sharing our narratives and experiences, we can dissipate ignorance and replace it with understanding and empathy.

Educatory Initiatives:
Regular workshops, seminars, and programs that focus on the vivid spectrum of human identities can play a significant role in dispelling myths and fostering mutual respect. This is particularly important in educational institutions, molding young minds to be more accepting and understanding.

Cultivating Safe Spaces

The Need for Refuge:
Everyone deserves an environment where they can be their authentic

selves without fear. Creating such safe spaces, both physical and virtual, is important in ensuring the mental and emotional well-being of individuals.

Guidelines and Ground Rules:
These safe spaces must be governed by guidelines that ensure respect, confidentiality, and understanding. Ground rules help in creating an environment where everyone feels valued and heard.

Taking Action: Standing Up for What's Right

Community Mobilization:
Grassroots movements, community programs, and support groups can be instrumental in addressing bullying at a local level. This bottom-up approach ensures that the solutions are tailored for the community's specific needs.

Legal Frameworks:
Advocacy plays a significant role in bringing about systemic change. By pushing for stringent anti-bullying laws and policies, we can create a safer environment for all, especially vulnerable populations.

Self-care and Healing

Journey Within:
Healing is as much an external process as it is internal. Engaging in self-reflection, meditation, and therapeutic practices can help in healing the wounds caused by bullying. Soundbaths, hypnotherapy, and spiritual baths with crystals or herbs are more non-invasive methods for cleansing and balancing one's energetic fields; creating the space needed for you mind and heart to heal.

Building a Support System:
Surrounding oneself with supportive friends, family, and professionals can significantly aid in the healing process. They act as reminders of our worth, our strength, and our potential. If you are not familiar with who would be the best type of support for your child or your child's friend, contact your local non-profit that centers focus on transgender and non-binary youth.

Reflective Questions:

1. How has a personal experience with bullying shaped your perspective

on acceptance?

2. How can proactive measures, like education, break the cycle of ignorance and bullying?

3. What role does community play in fostering acceptance and understanding?

Family Exercise: The Chain of Kindness

Objective: To create an environment of understanding and acceptance within the family unit.

Instructions:

1. Sit in a circle with family members.
2. One member shares an experience where they felt out of place or misunderstood. This could be due to their interests, appearance, or beliefs.
3. The next person shares how they can support or uplift the person who shared their story.
4. Continue the chain until everyone has had a turn.
5. Reflect on the interconnectedness of your stories and the impact of understanding and kindness.

By amplifying understanding, dispelling ignorance, and fostering environments of love and acceptance, we can effectively stand up against bullying and create communities where everyone's eccentricity is celebrated.

CHAPTER 14: ROLE MODELS: TRANSGENDER FIGURES IN MEDIA AND HISTORY

As we walk through the chronicles of history and the scrolls of the modern media landscape, we find individuals whose stories inspire, motivate, and provide hope. Their resilience, strength, and authenticity in embracing their truth is a testament to the indomitable spirit of humankind. My path as a non-religious transgender spiritual teacher has been illuminated by the guiding lights of these very role models. Their stories are our stories, teaching us to persevere and reminding us that we are never alone.

Historical Footprints

Ancient Voices: Transgender Histories before Modern Times

Exploring humanity, we have learned of civilizations across the globe who possess interconnected tales of transgender and non-binary individuals in their culture and history. These figures, often veiled in the mysteries of time, stood as symbols of power, spirituality, and transformation. They were testament to the spectrum of human existence, which never rigidly adhered to binary constructs.

Many transgender and non-binary individuals occupied societal centric roles. As we have learned, within many Indigenous American tribes, the 'Two-Spirit' individuals were seen as gifted; embracing both male and female spirits. Similarly, across the expansive lands of Africa and Asia, from the effeminate priests of ancient Nubia to gender-diverse roles among the Bugis people of Indonesia, these individuals were more than mere mortals; they were channels of deeper cosmic understanding.

However, with the march of empires, colonial influences, and the imposition of foreign religious beliefs, these figures were often sidelined, their roles diminished, and their histories erased or rewritten. The indigenous tales of respect and reverence were overshadowed by indoctrinated narratives of sin, abnormality, and deviance. As we dig deeper into the chronicles of time, these ancient voices resurface, reminding us that gender diversity isn't a modern phenomenon but a fundamental facet of humanity's abounding evolution.

From Erasure to Enlightenment: Rediscovering Transgender Histories

The stories of transgender and non-binary individuals, despite being age-old, experienced an era where they were muted, tucked away into the recesses of history's fading libraries. This dark age of erasure was marked by conquests, colonialism, and the widespread dissemination of monolithic beliefs. These narratives, seen as contradictory or abnormal, were strategically excluded from popular discourses or were twisted to fit into narratives that stripped them of their power, agency, and reverence.

However, the winds of change began to stir as societies entered eras of renaissance, reformation, and enlightenment. Intellectuals, historians, and scholars took it upon themselves to seek the truth, peeling back layers of imposed history to reveal the luminous tales of transgender and non-binary figures from the past. This process was neither swift nor easy. It involved relearning our internal power, unlearning false narratives, and constant confrontation with deeply embedded biases. Yet, the dedication to seeking truth and justice led to a revival of the true narratives, granting them the dignity and respect they had been denied for centuries.

In our age of smart technology and global connectivity, the journey from erasure to enlightenment continues to accelerate. With every unearthed artifact, translated manuscript, or oral history retold, the world gains a clearer understanding of the many expressions of gender experiences. Museums, educational institutions, and media platforms now embrace and amplify these stories, ensuring that future generations recognize and respect the deep roots and contributions of transgender and non-binary individuals throughout time.

Pioneers of Modern Times: The Torchbearers of Transgender Rights and Representation

1. Marsha P. Johnson - A central figure in the early LGBTQIA2S+ rights movement, Johnson, a Black transgender woman, played a key role in the events at the Stonewall Inn in 1969 which are often cited as the catalyst for the modern LGBTQIA2S+ rights movement. She also co-founded the Street Transvestite Action Revolutionaries (STAR) with Sylvia Rivera, providing shelter and support to homeless LGBTQIA2S+ youth.

2. Christine Jorgensen - Known for being the first American to become widely known for having sex reassignment surgery, Jorgensen's story brought international attention to transgender issues during the 1950s.

3. Billy Tipton - An American jazz musician, Tipton lived as a man for several decades, with many people unaware of his assigned gender at birth until his passing in 1989.

4. Miss Major Griffin-Gracy - An activist and community leader for transgender rights, particularly trans women of color, Miss Major's activism stretches back to the Stonewall era, and she continues to be an influential voice for incarcerated trans individuals.

5. Jan Morris - A renowned Welsh writer best known for her travel writings, Morris transitioned in the 1970s and wrote candidly about her experiences in her memoir "Conundrum."

6. Lucas Silveira - Lead singer of the Canadian rock band The Cliks, Silveira is one of the first openly transgender men to be signed to a major record label.

7. Laverne Cox - As an Emmy-nominated actress, Cox rose to fame on the show "Orange Is the New Black" and has since become a prominent advocate for transgender rights, especially for transgender women of color.

8. Geena Rocero - A Filipina-American model and activist, Rocero made waves when she came out as transgender during a TED talk in 2014. She founded Gender Proud, an advocacy organization focused on transgender rights.

9. Jazz Jennings - Gaining attention at a young age for her documentary, Jennings has become a role model for young transgender individuals. Her reality show, "I Am Jazz," chronicles her life and experiences as a

transgender teen and young adult.

10. Yance Ford - An Emmy-nominated director, Ford is known for his documentary "Strong Island." He made history as the first openly transgender man and the first Black openly transgender man to be nominated for an Academy Award.

11. Jamie Clayton - Actress and model, Clayton gained fame for her role in the Netflix series "Sense8." She has become an outspoken advocate for transgender representation in the entertainment industry.

12. Andrea Jenkins - As the first openly transgender Black woman elected to public office in the United States, Jenkins serves on the Minneapolis City Council. She is also a poet, educator, and activist, emphasizing the importance of political representation for marginalized communities.

13. Alok Vaid-Menon - A gender non-conforming writer, performer, and fashion icon, Alok has been a significant voice in addressing the complexities of gender through art and literature. Their work emphasizes the need for a more inclusive and intersectional approach to gender rights, merging activism with artistic expression.

14. Thomas Beatie - Often referred to as "The Pregnant Man," Beatie made international headlines when he became the first publicly known transgender man to become pregnant and give birth. His public discussion of his experiences challenged societal notions about pregnancy, gender roles, and parenthood.

15. Janet Mock - An American writer, television host, and transgender rights activist, Mock became a leading voice for transgender rights and representation after the release of her memoir "Redefining Realness." She has also been instrumental in increasing transgender representation in media, producing and writing for the TV series "Pose," which celebrates the ballroom culture of the '80s and '90s and the transgender community's role in it.

16. Phyllis Randolph Frye – American author and legal pioneer, Fry became the first openly transgender judge to be appointed in the United States. As the star feature in the book, "Phyllis Frye and the Fight for Transgender Rights", we are enlightened with the trials, struggles, and triumphs of Frye's early life and accounts of her rise through the legal, judicial, and political realms. Frye also founded the International Conference on Transgender Law and Employment Policy which helped

to change the landscape of transgender rights for all within and supporters of the trans community.

Recognizing the bravery and pioneering spirit of transgender children and their advocates is essential. Here are a few who have made significant contributions:

17. Jazz Jennings - Although already mentioned, it's worth reiterating that Jazz became a public figure as a transgender child. She co-wrote a children's book called "I Am Jazz," which is based on her own experiences, providing relatable content for other transgender children and a resource for schools and families.

18. Rebekah Bruesehoff - Rebekah has been a vocal advocate for transgender youth rights from a very young age. With the support of her family, she has spoken at rallies, participated in marches, and used her platform on social media to emphasize the importance of love and acceptance.

19. Desmond is Amazing (Desmond Napoles) - A drag kid and LGBTQIA2S+ community advocate, Desmond has been a beacon for self-expression and has brought attention to the importance of allowing children to explore and express their authentic selves. He's been a voice against bullying and a symbol of resilience.

20. Zaya Wade - Daughter of NBA star Dwyane Wade and actress Gabrielle Union, Zaya's public coming out as transgender brought discussions of transgender youth into mainstream media, sports, and popular culture. With her family's support, she's continued to shine a light on the experiences of transgender kids.

21. Kai Shappley - Kai, a transgender girl from Texas, has been at the center of discussions about transgender rights in schools. With a powerful voice, she's spoken before school boards and participated in documentaries, advocating for the rights of transgender students everywhere.

These young pioneers, along with their families, have played crucial roles in shifting public understanding and discourse surrounding transgender youth.

Transgender Culture in Global Contexts

At this stage in our wondrous journey, you understand that transgender individuals are not a new nor Western-centric phenomenon. Globally, their footprints have been forever enshrined in the historical records of early civilizations. From the Hijra of South Asia, who have a well-documented history spanning more than 4,000 years, to the "sworn virgins" of the Balkans, gender diversity is a Long Pao Dragon-robe full of striking patterns and colors. Even today, our energy continues to connect us with individuals still making history. As we speak, transgender and non-binary pioneers are pushing to educate and enlighten their community. Let us peer through the lens of those who understood that greatness is found in the inner strength you develop as a result of living your truth.

Brazil's Advocates:

Brazil! At the mere mention of the name we think of colorful festivals, invigorating music, Feijodas! Furthermore, therein lies a great passionate people, proud of their nation, who believe strongly in the power of the people. At times polarized, it is also known for its political struggles, freedom of expression, and its historical, elaborate relationship with gender and sexuality. On one hand, the nation boasts some of the largest LGBTQ celebrations in the world, like the São Paulo Pride Parade. Yet, simultaneously, Brazil grapples with alarming rates of violence against transgender individuals. Amidst this paradox, a wave of transgender advocates has risen, championing the cause of acceptance, rights, and visibility in a nation marked by its contrasts.

Transgender activists such as Laerte Coutinho, a renowned cartoonist, have utilized their platforms to challenge and disrupt traditional notions of gender within Brazilian society. Laerte's journey from a celebrated artist then coming out as a transgender woman was not without its challenges in the public eye. However, her transition and candid discussions about her experiences provided a much-needed representation and sparked national dialogues about gender identity and acceptance. Similarly, figures like Linn da Quebrada, a musician and actress, use art and media to highlight the narratives of transgender and queer communities, juxtaposing the revelry of Brazilian culture with poignant insights on the lived experiences of its marginalized individuals.

These advocates work tirelessly in a landscape where political, religious, and cultural forces often collide. The rise of conservative political factions has threatened the rights and safety of transgender Brazilians, but in the face of adversity, these resilient advocates continue to fight. Whether it's through legal battles, artistic expression, or grassroots movements, they strive to shape a future where every Brazilian, regardless of gender identity, can truly embrace the country's ethos of "alegria" (joy) without fear.

France: A Revolution of Identity and Expression

France, a land of artistry, philosophy, and revolution, has long been a canvas for those who challenge the norm and redefine the human experience. Just as the universe is ever-expanding, evolving in cosmic cycles of birth and rebirth, so too is the understanding of gender in this nation that has witnessed centuries of change. Here, transgender voices are rising, integrating new narratives into the lived consciousness of the people, reminding us that authenticity is an act of liberation.

One such voice is Océan, a filmmaker, comedian, and writer who brought the intimate details of his transition into the public eye with transparency and grace. His documentary series, Océan, became a portal into his journey, allowing audiences to see beyond the physical transformation and into the deeper energetic realignment of self. France has also witnessed the rise of Marie Cau, the country's first openly transgender mayor. With the dignity of a leader and the courage of a visionary, she shattered barriers, showing that transgender people do not merely exist on the fringes but are an essential force within society's structure.

Yet, the battle for true equity continues. France, despite its progressive image, still wrestles with outdated systems that fail to fully support transgender individuals, particularly in healthcare and legal recognition. But just as celestial bodies orbit in cycles of renewal, change is inevitable. Transgender advocates in France are cosmic catalysts, bringing forth an era where identity is honored in all its radiant forms, much like the constellations that shine across the ever expanding multiverse.

South Africa: Guardians of Truth and Resilience

Beneath the skies of South Africa, where the land hums with ancestral wisdom of the Orishas and the stars illuminate the path of seekers, transgender individuals are forging new realities. This is a nation that has known struggle and transformation, where history itself has been rewritten by those who refused to accept oppression as fate. In this place of raw power and deep spiritual connection, transgender advocates are carrying forward the same energy that once dismantled apartheid; an energy that recognizes that freedom must be afforded to all.

Yaya Mavundla, a transgender activist and media figure, stands as one of the beacons of this movement. Through her work in fashion, media, and activism, she embodies the fusion of visibility and empowerment, using her presence to challenge societal norms and uplift those who walk a similar path. Leigh Ann Van Der Merwe, founder of the Social, Health, and Empowerment Feminist Collective, dedicates her energy to supporting Black transgender women, whose struggles are often compounded by economic and racial inequalities. These women, like celestial bodies locked in a gravitas dance of resilience, move forward against gravitational forces of discrimination, their light impossible to ignore.

Though South Africa's constitution explicitly protects LGBTQIA2S+ rights, the lived experiences of transgender individuals remain riddled with hardship. From accessing affirming healthcare to facing violence in both rural and urban spaces, the journey is far from over. Yet, just as the cosmos continues to expand, so too does the consciousness of a nation that has proven its ability to evolve. With each transgender voice that rises, South Africa edges closer to a future where freedom is not conditional but an undeniable birthright.

Ireland: Awakening the Soul of a Nation

Ireland, a land steeped in myth and magic, is no stranger to transformation. Once bound by the constraints of rigid tradition, it has emerged as a nation willing to confront its past and embrace new ways of being. As the rivers carve their paths through the emerald hills, so too have transgender individuals carved their space within the progressing narrative of Irish identity. Their presence, their resilience, and their insistence on visibility have become substantiated roots in the ever-growing awareness of gender diversity.

Dr. Lydia Foy is one such luminary, a transgender woman whose legal battle for recognition paved the way for the Gender Recognition Act of 2015. Following her gender change operation she requested a change to her birth certificate to reflect her correct gender. Initially denied, she battled the legal system for 22-years and was finally successful in receiving her corrected legal documents. Her persistence forced the Irish government to acknowledge the rights of transgender individuals, ensuring that identity could no longer be dictated by outdated laws. Meanwhile, TENI (Transgender Equality Network Ireland) works tirelessly to educate, support, and uplift the trans community, ensuring that no one walks this journey alone.

Despite these victories, Ireland still carries echoes of its past. Transgender healthcare remains inaccessible for many, and social acceptance, though growing, still meets resistance in certain corners of society. But Ireland is a land of storytellers, and the story of its transgender community is far from finished. With each chapter written in courage and truth, the nation is awakening, shedding its old skin, and stepping into a new age where gender diversity is embraced as part of the soul of its people

Canada: The Northern Lights of Inclusion and Activism

Amidst the brilliance of the Northern Lights, Canada is often seen as a sanctuary for LGBTQIA2S+ individuals, a nation that prides itself on inclusivity and progress. Yet, like all places in this Earthly realm, there exists a duality, a contrast between policy and reality, between protection and the lived experiences of transgender individuals who still face barriers despite legal advancements.

One of Canada's most influential transgender figures is Vivian Namaste, an academic whose research has shed light on the experiences of transgender sex workers and marginalized communities. Through her work, she dismantles misconceptions and challenges institutions to recognize the complexities of transgender lives. Another trailblazer, Rupert Raj, has been a force of advocacy since the 1970s, creating networks of support and visibility long before society was willing to acknowledge the struggles of transgender individuals.

While Canada offers gender-affirming healthcare and legal recognition, disparities remain. Similar to their United States counterparts, Indigenous Two-Spirit individuals often face compounded discrimination, navigating both the systemic challenges of colonialism and the barriers of transphobia. Organizations such as Egale Canada and The Enchanté Network continue to push for equity, ensuring that no one is left behind in the pursuit of dignity and respect. Canada, with its intimate connection to nature and ever-expanding consciousness, is a reminder that progress is an ongoing journey. The stars do not stop shining once they are seen; they continue to burn, illuminating the way forward.

As transgender voices continue to shape Canada's social landscape, the nation stands as an example of progress that is still evolving. The lessons from its advocates remind us that laws alone do not guarantee equality, true justice is achieved through continuous effort, education, and the unwavering courage of those who stand in their truth.

Throughout this material real, transgender individuals rise, their voices still echoing across time and space, vibrating, aligned with universal frequencies. From the pulsating rhythms of Brazil to the revolutionary spirit of France, from the unbreakable will of South Africa to the evolving soul of Ireland and the steadfast activism of Canada, each story is a testament to the infinite ways in which gender, identity, and existence manifest.

Media: A Double-Edged Sword

Spotlighting Authentic Narratives

If history has enlightened our minds with anything, it would be the necessity of representation. The importance of authentic narratives cannot be understated. For decades, the stories of transgender individuals were filtered through the lenses of those unfamiliar with the lived experiences of this community. These representations, often rooted in stereotypes, misconceptions, or just blatant lies, not only did a disservice to the community by portraying them inaccurately but also perpetuated harmful biases in the larger society. As media wields a considerable influence on societal perceptions, the necessity for genuine portrayals, stories told by and for transgender individuals, became paramount.

With the rise of independent media platforms and a push for diverse voices in mainstream media, there's been a noticeable shift towards authentic storytelling. Transgender writers, filmmakers, and artists are stepping into the limelight, ensuring their tales are shared without dilution or misinterpretation. Shows like "Pose," with its groundbreaking casting and genuine exploration of the New York ballroom culture, or writers like Janet Mock and Imogen Binnie, who expertly delivered an in-depth look into the nuances of transgender experiences in their works, have significantly transformed the narrative terrain. Filled with complexities, joys, struggles, and triumphs, their artistry offer viewers and readers a genuine insight into their world, reshaping preconceived notions and fostering genuine empathy.

> Several renowned narratives expressed through media are "Paris is Burning" (1990), "Major" (2015), "Mama Gloria" (2020), "Still Black: A Portrait of a Black Transman" (2008), "The Death and Life of Marsha P. Johnson" (2017), "Kumu Hina" (2014), and "Passing" (short, 2015).

However, while strides have been made, the journey towards full representation is ongoing. The need to spotlight authentic narratives extends beyond just media to education, policies, and everyday conversations. Undiluted, genuine voices serve as powerful tools for change, bridging gaps of understanding.

Challenges and Misrepresentations:

The journey towards true understanding and acceptance of the transgender community is fraught with numerous challenges, many of which stem from long-standing misrepresentations. Historically, the media landscape was rife with depictions of transgender individuals that leaned heavily into stereotypes, painting them as deceptive, mentally unstable, or merely as the punchline to cruel jokes; such as with "Ace Ventura – Pet Detective". These types of portrayals not only muffled the authentic voices and experiences of transgender individuals but also entrenched harmful biases within the societal psyche. The ripple effects of these portrayals have had severe implications, from stigmatizing the community to fostering environments where fetishes, discrimination, abuse and even murder thrives; especially amongst the Black trans-feminine demographic.

These skewed representations have done more than just perpetuate falsehoods. They've built barriers. For many transgender individuals, navigating the world becomes a minefield, with every step shadowed by the weight of these misconceptions. The misrepresentations contribute to challenges in healthcare, where transgender individuals might encounter professionals ill-equipped or unwilling to address their specific needs. They feed into legislative battles, where rights are debated based on outdated or false notions. In everyday interactions, they breed misunderstandings, where individuals are forced to contend with the challenge of constantly debunking myths or justifying their identity.

However, in the face of these challenges, there's also resilience. The transgender community, allies, and advocates have consistently rallied against misrepresentations, pushing for more accurate, compassionate, and diverse portrayals in all spheres of society. While the journey is ongoing, every corrected narrative or debunked myth brings society a step closer to understanding, empathy, and genuine acceptance.

The Importance of Relatable Role Models

Seeing One's Self:

We all have dreams of grander; there's a true yearning embedded within us all: the desire to see oneself reflected in the world around us. This longing isn't merely for vanity or affirmation; it's a deeply human need to belong, to know that one's existence is acknowledged, valued, and understood. For the transgender community, this reflection has, for far too long, been a murky and distorted image, filled more with societal prejudices than sincere understanding. However, the power of truly seeing oneself - in media, literature, leadership roles, and daily life - can be transformative, offering true solace.

The moments in which transgender individuals can see authentic reflections of themselves are not just fundamental for personal growth, but they also become collective milestones. A transgender child reading about an activist who shares their journey, or a teenager seeing a transgender actor playing a multifaceted role on screen, isn't just consuming content. They're witnessing a world where they fit, where their dreams, challenges, and joys are recognized. These moments shatter feelings of isolation, replacing them with a sense of community, connection, and possibility. As of 2022, studies reflect there are approximately 300,000 children under the age of 18 who identify as transgender. Of this community, 86% of our youth have expressing that they've considered unaliving themselves with 56% reporting that they have previously attempted to unalive themselves.[45] These figures are predicted to rise as a result of the 2024 US presidential election; where the winning candidate signed executive orders to eliminate mental and medical care for transgender youth and adults. However, groups, such as the ACLU (American Civil Liberties Union) are relentless in their fight against the political administration to restore rights of dignity and respect to the transgender community.

It is apparent that the quest for representation is more than just seeking mirrors; it's about building windows. When authentic transgender stories and experiences are shared, they not only resonate with those within the community but also become enlightening windows for the wider society. They provide insights, foster empathy, and challenge entrenched biases. As the world continues to evolve, ensuring that every individual truly sees themselves becomes not just an ideal to strive for but a responsibility and a testament to our shared humanity.

Inspiration for the Next Generation:

Each generation is influenced by the tales, triumphs, and tribulations of those who came before. The narratives of resilience, determination, and authenticity from the transgender community serve as a guiding star for the next generation. They shine brightly, not just as a testament to what has been

---

[45] Austin A, Craig SL, D'Souza S, McInroy LB. Suicidality Among Transgender Youth: Elucidating the Role of Interpersonal Risk Factors [published correction appears in J Interpers Violence. 2020 Jul 29:886260520946128. doi: 10.1177/0886260520946128]. J Interpers Violence. 2022;37(5-6):NP2696-NP2718. doi:10.1177/0886260520915554

overcome, but as a beacon of hope for what the future can hold. As the stories of transgender pioneers, activists, and everyday heroes continue to unfurl, they inspire younger generations to dream big, stand tall, and embrace their true selves with unyielding pride.

The impact of these narratives extends beyond just providing a roadmap. They instill a sense of belonging, anchoring young transgender individuals in a community full of shared experiences and collective strength. Every tale of adversity surmounted, every barrier broken, and every voice that rises above the din of discrimination serves as a potent reminder: they are not alone in their journey. With each shared story, seeds of inspiration are sown, germinating into powerful aspirations, ambitions, and actions that have the potential to shape the world.

But inspiration isn't a one-way street. The energy, creativity, and relentless spirit of the next generation also inspires older generations. They bring fresh perspectives, innovative solutions, and a renewed passion to continue the work that has been started. As they stand on the shoulders of those who paved the way, they also extend a hand, ensuring that the chain of inspiration remains unbroken, propelling the world towards greater inclusivity, understanding, and love.

Reflective Questions:

1. How have transgender role models in media and history influenced your understanding and perspective?
2. Why is it important for the media to provide accurate and positive representation?
3. Can you think of a moment where a story or a figure deeply resonated with you? Why?

Family Exercise: Exploring Narratives

Objective: To understand and appreciate the diverse experiences of transgender individuals through history and media.

Instructions:

1. Together as a family, choose a documentary, movie, or series episode that focuses on the life of a transgender individual or historical figure.
2. After watching, discuss the feelings, challenges, and triumphs portrayed.
3. Reflect on how these stories mirror broader societal narratives and how

they can influence perceptions.

Through the diverse spheres of their lives, these role models extend a hand, guiding us forward, reminding us of our worth, and emphasizing the importance of forging paths filled with authenticity and love.

CHAPTER 15: SUPPORTING FRIENDS: HOW TO BE AN ALLY

Developing empathy as a result of walking in the truth of transgender and non-binary experiences can sometimes feel overwhelming; especially for parents who want to guide their children with love, understanding, and knowledge. I've walked the path of self-discovery and recognition, and I've learned the value of having allies by my side. The passage towards understanding is a shared one, and with each step, we come closer to creating a world where everyone feels appreciated and accepted.

For guardians and parents, teaching children about being allies to their transgender friends is a crucial step toward a more inclusive tomorrow. Here's how you can foster this spirit of alliance within your young ones:

1. Begin with a Story: Children resonate with stories. Share age-appropriate narratives about transgender individuals. This helps them understand and relate better. Over time, stories will lay a foundation of empathy and understanding.

2. Teach Active Listening: Empower your child to listen when their friends share personal experiences. Being heard is a powerful affirmation. By teaching our kids to listen, we're fostering a culture of respect and validation.

3. Emphasize the Power of Words: Teach your child about pronouns and the significance of using correct names. Make them understand that just as they wouldn't like being called by a different name, it's essential to

respect others' identities.

4. Role-Playing Activities: Engage in role-playing exercises at home. Let your child assume the role of a friend who's trying to understand a transgender classmate. This interactive method reinforces empathy and helps them navigate real-life scenarios.

5. Celebrate Differences: Highlight the beauty in diversity. Just as we have different cultures, religions, and tastes, we also have varied gender identities. Teach them that these differences make our world vibrant and colorful.

6. Encourage Questions: Children are naturally curious. Instead of shushing their questions, encourage them. If there's something you don't know, it's a learning opportunity for both of you. Dive into resources, books, or even seek guidance from experts like counselors or teachers.

7. Lead by Example: Children often mirror adult behaviors. When they see you interacting positively and inclusively with transgender individuals or speaking up against prejudice, they learn.

8. Encourage Inclusivity in Play: Foster inclusivity in their playtime. Books, toys, and games that portray diverse characters, including transgender ones, can be a powerful tool.

9. Address Mistakes Gracefully: If your child makes an error, such as misgendering someone, correct them gently. Instead of reprimanding, turn it into a learning experience. Here's a gentle approach to guide your child:

> A. Start with Basics:
> Before addressing misgendering, ensure your child has a basic understanding of gender identities. Using age-appropriate language, explain that while many people identify as either boys or girls, some people might identify as neither or both. And it's essential to call people what they prefer to be called, just as it's crucial to get a friend's name right.
>
> B. Use Analogies:
> Children often grasp complex ideas better when related to their personal experiences. You can say, "Imagine if everyone called you by your brother's or sister's name even after you corrected them. It wouldn't feel good, right? That's how it feels when we don't use the

right gender for someone."

C. Address the Moment:
If a misgendering incident occurs, address it soon after the fact. You might say, "I noticed you called Taylor 'he' earlier. Taylor prefers 'she'." Then, provide a moment for reflection, asking how they might feel if someone repeatedly referred to them incorrectly.

D. Practice Correct Pronouns Together:
Repetition aids memory. If your child has mistakenly used the wrong pronoun for someone, practice the correct pronoun together. For instance, "Taylor is going to bring her ball tomorrow, so she and you can play together."

E. Share Stories:
Read books or share stories that depict diverse gender identities. When children see characters being misgendered and then correctly gendered, it creates a blueprint for them.

F. Emphasize Apologizing and Moving On:
Teach your child that if they misgender someone, a simple apology without making a big fuss is the best approach. "Excuse me, I meant 'she'," and then continue the conversation. An "I'm sorry" or an "I apologize" would work just as effectively.

G. Address Persistent Misgendering:
If misgendering continues, it might be beneficial to have a more in-depth conversation. There might be confusion or misconceptions that need to be addressed.

H. Praise Efforts:
When you notice your child making an effort to use the correct pronouns, offer praise. Positive reinforcement can go a long way.

Remember, the goal isn't to instill fear of making mistakes but to cultivate understanding and respect. With patience and guidance, children can learn the significance of using correct pronouns and the impact it has on fostering inclusive and loving communities.

We are teaching our children to be allies. This is not indoctrination. Indoctrination is the act of imposing a rigid set of beliefs onto someone without space for inquiry, personal discovery, or critical thinking. It demands compliance rather than understanding; obedience rather than exploration.

Teaching children about the existence of transgender and non-binary people, however, is not indoctrination, it is education. It is the same as teaching them about different cultures, religions, and the beautiful expressions of humanity that exist across time and space.

To acknowledge the reality of transgender lives is not to force an identity upon a child, but to offer them the wisdom to approach the world with empathy and respect. The multiverse itself is limitless, constantly expanding, much like our knowledge and awareness. Just as we teach our young ones that the stars stretch beyond what the eye can see, we teach them that gender is not confined to a single form; that it moves, flows, and radiates through individuals in countless ways. To withhold this truth, to deny them the understanding of the diverse souls they share this existence with, would be to limit their connection to the infinite possibilities of love, acceptance, and human connection.

Teaching respect for transgender people is not indoctrination; it is an act of opening the heart, expanding the mind, and aligning with the ever-unfolding nature of our world.

We aren't just helping them shape their worldview but also planting seeds for a future where acceptance and love override prejudice and ignorance. The beauty of teaching about alliance is that it doesn't just stop with understanding transgender topics. It becomes a life lesson about respect, love, and unity in diversity.

Our children are the hope for a brighter, kinder tomorrow. And with the right guidance, they will not only become allies to their transgender friends but also torchbearers of acceptance for all.

Reflective Questions:

1. Self-awareness: Think back to a time when you might have inadvertently misgendered someone or felt unsure about their pronouns. How did you handle the situation? What could you have done differently?

2. Empathy: Imagine how it might feel to be constantly referred to in a way that doesn't resonate with your internal sense of self. How would you want your friends and family to support you?

3. Openness: Reflect on any initial resistances or discomforts you might feel when talking about gender diversity. What might be the source of

these feelings?

4. Education: What are some areas about transgender issues that you feel you need to learn more about?

5. Action: Think about the steps you've taken so far to be an ally to transgender individuals. What more can you do in your day-to-day life?

Family Exercises: Walk a Mile in Their Shoes

Objective: To work through some exercises aimed at giving you a more in depth look into the seeing from someone else's point of view.

Instructions:

1. Pronoun Practice: Spend an evening where everyone in the family chooses a different pronoun, even if it doesn't align with their gender identity. This is not to make light of transgender experiences but to foster understanding through experiential learning. At the end of the evening, discuss how it felt to be addressed differently.

2. Story Time: Invest in books that discuss gender diversity. Read these books together and discuss the stories. A good start might be books that feature non-binary or transgender characters.

3. Role Play: Set up scenarios where one family member might inadvertently misgender another. Practice how to apologize and move forward. Role-playing helps in building confidence in real-life situations.

4. Education Night: Dedicate a family night to watch documentaries or educational videos about transgender experiences. After watching, hold a discussion about what everyone learned and felt.

5. Ally Challenge: As a family, come up with a list of actionable steps you can all take over the month to be better allies. This might include activities like attending a local LGBTQIA2S+ event, setting up a fundraiser for transgender rights organizations, or inviting a speaker to a community event.

6. Expression Day: Hold a day where everyone in the family can express their gender in any way they feel. There are no rights or wrongs. Discuss the feelings and experiences at the end of the day.

7. Language Awareness: Over dinner or during a designated discussion time, talk about the language related to transgender issues. Discuss words or terms that are new, words that are considered outdated or offensive, and the importance of language in showing respect.

Remember, the goal of these exercises is to create a safe space for learning, understanding, and growth. Mistakes may happen, but they can be wonderful opportunities for learning.

CHAPTER 16: FAMILIES WITH TRANSGENDER MEMBERS: LOVE AND ACCEPTANCE

I am ever inspired by the stories of families embracing their transgender members. Families, whether related by blood or not, form the very core of society, and when acceptance radiates within them, it creates a ripple effect that can bring about meaningful change in our world.

I am fully aware of the extraordinary challenges and triumphs faced by our community. But before explaining some practices and perspectives, I want to make you aware that your desire to understand and your quest for knowledge already speaks volumes of your love and commitment.

The Energy of Acceptance

The true essence of a family lies in its unwavering love and support; its ability to become the sanctuary one retreats to, especially in times of vulnerability. As I've journeyed both personally and spiritually, I've come to recognize that acceptance is the glue that sustains this sanctuary. Acceptance is not tolerance; it's a thoughtful acknowledgment, a deep sense of belonging that helps to formulate the very core of another's existence.

For transgender and non-binary individuals, tolerance is a hidden danger because of its passive nature. It is an acknowledgment of existence without true recognition, a hesitant nod that says, I will allow you to be here, but I do not celebrate your presence. It is an energy that keeps transgender souls at arm's length, making them feel like outsiders, as though their existence is something to be endured rather than embraced. The weight of mere tolerance can be deeply damaging to transgender individuals, particularly within their own families. Research published in the Journal of Adolescent Health found that transgender youth who experience family rejection or only conditional acceptance face significantly higher risks of depression, anxiety, and suicidal ideation[46].

When a loved one unveils their transgender identity, they're inviting you into a sacred space, one that they've held close, sometimes shielded, and often pondered over for many moments in solitude. When someone is merely tolerated in their own home, their spirit absorbs that energy, internalizing the idea that they are a burden, that their identity is something to be managed rather than celebrated. Over time, this dissonance creates emotional wounds that can manifest as self-doubt, low self-worth, and even physical symptoms of stress-related illnesses.

This sharing and acceptance of their identity becomes the bedrock of trust. And trust, once established, transforms the familial bond, making it unbreakable, adaptable, and resilient. It paves the way for deeper connections, more meaningful interactions, and an unspoken understanding that no matter the journey's twists and turns, the family remains a cohesive, accepting unit. Such is the power and beauty of genuine acceptance within a family. True acceptance is an energy that aligns with the great celestial flow of love and interconnectedness. It reflects the way the universe welcomes all beings without question, how the stars shine upon every planet without discrimination.

The Fluidity of Transition

The journey of transition is not a straight path, but rather more like a flowing river, shifting with time, experience, and self-discovery. It is sometimes steady and sometimes unpredictable. There are moments of extreme joy, where a transgender person sees themselves reflected in the world as they've always felt inside. There are also moments of deep introspection, where emotions rise like tides, revealing the weight of societal expectations, family dynamics, and personal evolution. It is important to understand that transition is not just about physical change. It is also an energetic shift, a spiritual alignment, a return to one's true self.

Families who wish to support their transgender loved ones can start by

---

[46] Ryan C, Russell ST, Huebner D, Diaz R, Sanchez J. Family acceptance in adolescence and the health of LGBT young adults. J Child Adolesc Psychiatr Nurs. 2010;23(4):205-213. doi:10.1111/j.1744-6171.2010.00246.x

relating to their own experiences of change. Transition is not exclusive to transgender individuals. Believe it or not, it is a universal experience that all humans navigate in different forms. A person who changes careers after decades in one field must rediscover their sense of purpose. A parent adjusting to an empty nest must redefine their role in the world. A child growing into adolescence must find comfort in their evolving identity. These experiences, while different from gender transition, all carry the same undercurrent; the uncertainty, growth, and the need for support. In recognizing this, families can connect to their transgender loved ones not as outsiders to change, but as fellow travelers through transformation.

Support in transition is not about having all the answers but about showing up with an open heart. We have found that transgender individuals with supportive family environments significantly increase ones quality of life.[47] This can be as simple as using the correct name and pronouns, standing up against transphobic remarks, or offering a listening ear when challenges arise. These acts, no matter how small they may seem, create that sanctuary of safety we have been mentioning.

Above all, family members must remember that transition is not just about the transgender person, it is a collective journey. As the person transitioning steps into their authentic self, those who love them are invited to step into deeper understanding, into a higher vibration of love. The universe thrives on change; the stars shift, galaxies expand, and energy transforms endlessly. In embracing the fluidity of transition, families align themselves with the natural flow of existence, where love and acceptance become the guiding forces that transcend all barriers.

Embracing Spiritual Teachings

In every deep belly breath, in every movement of the stars, the universe reminds us that change is the quintessence of existence. Just as galaxies expand and evolve, so too must our hearts and minds grow to embrace the divine nature of all beings, including our transgender and non-binary family members. Spiritual and energy healing teachings offer a pathway to this understanding, not by forcing belief, but by opening the soul to the frequency of unconditional love. Rituals of healing, whether through soundbaths, breath, movement, or meditation, can create a sacred space for families to deepen their connection, release past conditioning, and step into a higher vibration of acceptance.

---

[47] Simons L, Schrager SM, Clark LF, Belzer M, Olson J. Parental support and mental health among transgender adolescents. J Adolesc Health. 2013;53(6):791-793. doi:10.1016/j.jadohealth.2013.07.019

I will continue to remind you that when your family member transitions, it is not just their journey; it is an energetic shift that invites everyone around them to evolve. Many spiritual traditions emphasize that true enlightenment comes not from clinging to what we have been taught, but from expanding our awareness beyond our limitations.

If the teachings you have followed instruct you to reject, harm, or condemn a transgender loved one, it may be time to seek wisdom from a different well. The soul is not bound to one book, one doctrine, nor one way of knowing. To truly embody love, we must be willing to explore teachings that uplift and honor all beings. This may mean studying other spiritual traditions, engaging in energy healing practices like Reiki and sound therapy, or simply listening to the experiences of transgender individuals with an open heart.

The foundation of any spiritual path is love, and love begins within. Individuals who practice self-compassion are more likely to show empathy and acceptance toward others[48]. This means that before we can offer love and understanding to others, we must first cultivate it within ourselves. Self-reflection, forgiveness, and personal healing are crucial steps in learning to support a transgender family member with true acceptance. When we align with love, when we release fear, we become vessels of divine harmony, capable of holding space for the transformation of those we cherish.

The universe does not demand conformity; it thrives in diversity. Living amongst the endless manifestations of life on Earth we bare witness to the beauty of difference. Families who embrace this truth will find that supporting their transgender loved ones is not an act of burden, but an act of spiritual awakening. It is a chance to move beyond outdated paradigms and step into the higher frequency of unconditional love; a love that exists beyond gender, beyond the physical, beyond all limitations.

Guiding Younger Siblings

When your family member shares their transgender or non-binary identity, the flow of change extends to everyone, including younger siblings. For some, this shift is met with curiosity and excitement. It's an opportunity to learn and grow alongside their loved one. For others, it can bring confusion, questions, or even fear of how their relationship might change.

---

[48] Neff KD, Germer CK. A pilot study and randomized controlled trial of the mindful self-compassion program. J Clin Psychol. 2013;69(1):28-44. doi:10.1002/jclp.21923

They may feel a sense of loss for the sibling they once knew, struggle to adjust to a new name and pronouns, or worry about how their family dynamics will evolve. Younger children, still learning about the world, may not yet have the words to express their emotions, but they will feel the energy of transformation within the home.

Siblings play an essential role in a transgender person's journey. They are often the first friends, the first confidants, and the first protectors. The love and acceptance of a sibling can be a powerful force, creating a safe and affirming space even when the outside world is less understanding. A supportive sibling can correct pronouns, stand up against bullying, and remind their transgender sibling that they are not alone. This bond, strengthened by unconditional love, mirrors the harmony of our planetary solar system. At times tumultuous, yet rhythmically bound to one another; energetically nourishing each other, shining brighter together.

Parents and guardians can guide younger siblings through this transition by nurturing open and honest communication. Encourage them to ask questions and express their emotions without fear of judgment. Provide them with age-appropriate resources to help them understand what it means to be transgender. This can be in the form of coloring books and movies and publications with transgender children as the main characters. Most importantly, reinforce that love is constant, that their sibling is still the same soul, merely stepping more fully into their truth. Children who grow up in environments that encourage open dialogue and emotional expression develop greater empathy and adaptability[49]. When we teach children that change is a natural and beautiful part of life, we align them with the wisdom of the multiverse itself. By nurturing a space of openness, parents help siblings become allies, strengthening the bonds of love that transcend labels and physical form.

Building Bridges with Extended Family

The ancestry of a family are layered with generations of various relationship; parents, siblings, and, crucially, the extended family. Grandparents, aunts, uncles, cousins, and close family friends all play significant roles in our 'stages of life'. Extended family members, harness and emit energy of varying frequencies; each carrying their own beliefs, histories, and emotions. When a family member transitions, these relatives may experience a range of feelings, from confusion and concern to unconditional

---

[49] Sharpe D, Rossiter L. Siblings of children with a chronic illness: a meta-analysis. J Pediatr Psychol. 2002;27(8):699-710. doi:10.1093/jpepsy/27.8.699

love and support. Some may embrace this shift with open hearts, while others may struggle with societal conditioning, personal biases, or a lack of understanding. Similar to parents and siblings, they may grieve who they thought their relative was, not realizing that nothing has been lost, only revealed. We must be willing and able to release our time-honored traditions in order to expedite our internal growth.

Parents and guardians play important roles in bridging this understanding. Introducing a transgender or non-binary child to extended family requires intention, patience, and care. Before any conversation takes place, it may be helpful to educate relatives on what it means to be transgender, addressing myths and misconceptions with facts and personal stories. Choose a time when emotions are calm, ensuring a safe environment where discussion can happen without fear or immediate rejection. Approach these moments with compassion but also with clear boundaries; affirming that this is not a debate, but a reality that deserves respect.

Sometimes, writing a heartfelt letter or sending educational resources before a face-to-face conversation can offer relatives time to process and reflect.

For transgender and non-binary children, safety and emotional well-being must always come first. If extended family members respond with negativity or rejection, parents must serve as guardians; not only of their children's physical space but of their spirit. Limit interactions with those who refuse to respect their identity, and reinforce messages of love and affirmation at home.

I reiterate, family is not defined by blood, but by the energy of love, safety, and acceptance. If certain relatives choose not to support, children must be reminded that they are still surrounded by family; those who stand beside them in love, whether related by lineage or by choice.

For extended family members who wish to be supportive but are unsure how, just start with the basics - listen, learn, and love. Use the correct name and pronouns, stand up for them in conversations, and seek to understand rather than judge. Ask thoughtful questions, not out of skepticism, but out of genuine curiosity and care.

Do not ask predatory questions. If you would not want a person asking the same question of your child, then it is likely not a fair question to ask of your transgender relative, regardless of their age. In addition, be patient with yourself as you unlearn old beliefs, just as you would want patience if you were learning a new language. You aren't just simply accepting a family member, you are stepping into a higher frequency of connection, aligning with the universal truth that every being is divine in their authenticity. When families embrace this understanding, they do more than support one person, they elevate the entire family consciousness, interconnecting high vibrational frequencies.

However, it's essential to remember that while education and open dialogue can build bridges, the journey to acceptance is deeply personal. It might take time for some extended family members to come around, and that decision should be left up to the individual. The key is to remain dedicated in love and support for the transgender family member while providing resources, time, and space for others to evolve. Through patience, love, and understanding, the broader family network can be transformed into a fortress of support.

Reflective Questions:

1. Think back to when you first learned about your family member's transgender identity. What were your initial feelings, and how have they evolved?
2. How has your understanding of gender changed since then?
3. In what ways can you further support your transgender family member during their journey?

Family Exercises: Building Stronger Connections

Objective: Using team building exercises aimed at building a foundation of understanding on common ground.

Instructions:

1. Memory Sharing: Sit together as a family and share fond memories involving the transgender family member. This activity emphasizes the essence of the person rather than their gender.
2. Family Vision Board: Create a vision board filled with positive affirmations, hopes for the future, and photographs that celebrate family unity and acceptance.
3. Resource Night: Dedicate an evening to explore books, documentaries, or articles on transgender experiences. Discuss them afterward, focusing on love, acceptance, and understanding.

Every family's journey will be unique, but rooted in love and understanding, any challenges can be transformed into moments of significant growth. Remember always to lead with love. It's the most potent tool you have.

CHAPTER 17: FINDING COMMON GROUND: NAVIGATING RESISTANCE WITHIN THE FAMILY

In every family, personalities of every facet exists. Differing beliefs, and attitudes bind together the volumes of shared experiences. It's the very diversity of these pieces that make families exceptional, colorful, and at times, challenging to navigate. As we tread along on the path of understanding and embrace transgender topics, we learn of the many paths strewn with resistance; areas where the transgender community is confronted by family members who hold hostile views. Personally, I've treaded this path and now aim to provide insight, guidance, and hope for families grappling with such challenges.

The Roots of Resistance

Consideration is the first step towards real transformation. You must consider the possibility that you just might be misguided about transgender people. Many times, hostility arises from a place of ignorance, misconceptions, or fear. For some, their beliefs are anchored in cultural, religious, or generational teachings that have defined gender in rigid, binary terms. For others, their apprehensions might be wrapped in the fear of the unknown or simple misunderstanding. Recognizing where this hostility originates is crucial in addressing it effectively.

Compassionate Conversations

Meeting hostility with anger is tempting, but as a spiritual guide, I advocate for a different approach: compassion. When confronted with a hostile family member, try to initiate a heart-to-heart conversation. Share personal stories, discuss scientific and sociological understandings, and even offer literature or documentaries that might shed light on transgender experiences. But above all, express the love, the hopes, and the dreams that remain unchanged regardless of gender identity. By humanizing the experience, you can gently challenge and reshape their perceptions.

Setting Boundaries

While it's vital to approach resistance with understanding and empathy, it's equally important to set clear boundaries. Your home and family should be a haven of love, acceptance, and respect. If a family member continually expresses hostility or refuses to respect your child's gender identity, it might be necessary to limit interactions or set ground rules.

Sometimes, a physical reminder can reinforce boundaries. Consider creating a family charter, where everyone contributes to writing down the key boundaries agreed upon. This can be hung in a communal area as a reminder. Alternatively, symbols or colors can be used; for instance, a specific colored light or sign on a bedroom door might signal that someone needs alone time and shouldn't be disturbed. Remember, it's not about alienation; it's about protection, love, and nurturing a positive environment for your child.

Encourage Group Learning

Consider hosting or attending group sessions focused on understanding transgender topics. Sometimes, hearing the perspectives of others, especially from individuals who've had transformative journeys from hostility to acceptance, can be powerful. Group settings also foster a community of support and collective learning.

The Power of Patience

Change doesn't happen overnight. While some family members might never fully understand or accept, many can evolve with time, exposure, and continuous engagement. Celebrate small shifts in perspective, and remain patient, offering resources and love consistently.

In conclusion, confronting hostility within one's family is one of the hardest challenges on this journey. However, with love, patience, and informed conversation, transformation is possible. As families, we have an inherent bond that transcends differences, and with effort, even the most rigid views can be softened, opening pathways to deeper understanding and love. Understand, the only goal isn't just acceptance; it's also to help create a family collage that celebrates every image, no matter how different.

Reflective Questions:

1. Introspection on Origins: Ask yourself, where do your beliefs and attitudes about gender and transgender topics originate from? Are they from personal experiences, cultural norms, religious teachings, or something else?

2. Empathy Exercise: Try to put yourself in the shoes of a transgender individual. Imagine the courage it takes to live authentically, especially in the face of misunderstanding or hostility. How would you want to be treated by your family?

3. Evaluation of Environment: Is your home environment one of unconditional love and acceptance? Are there areas or situations where it might not feel that way for everyone?

4. Relationship Prioritization: Think of your relationship with the family member showing resistance. Apart from this topic, what binds you two? Can that bond be a starting point for building understanding?

Family Exercises: Empathy Steps: Walking another Mile or So in Their Shoes

Objective: To foster understanding, compassion, and open dialogue within families, helping them unite and support their transgender members."

Instructions:

1. Ground Rule Establishment: As a family, create a list of ground rules for discussions around sensitive topics. This can provide a structured and safe space for everyone to voice their opinions without fear.

2. Community Engagement: Attend community events or support groups that focus on transgender awareness and inclusion. Meeting and interacting with a diverse group of people can be an eye-opener for many.

3. Book Club Approach: Choose a book that deals with transgender topics, experiences, or stories. Read it collectively as a family and hold weekly discussions about the chapters, sharing insights and learning from

each other.

By engaging in these reflective exercises and activities, families can pave the way for deeper understanding, mutual respect, and lasting acceptance. It's a journey of growth for everyone involved.

CHAPTER 18: CHALLENGES AND TRIUMPHS: REAL-LIFE SCENARIOS

Life is intertwined with stories - tales of struggles, moments of epiphanies, and the triumphs that follow. For transgender individuals and those who love them, these stories are particularly important. They provide a beacon of light, hope, and sometimes, a cautionary tale to guide others. Along this empathic transcendence, we've encountered brave souls that chose to share personal narratives to showcase the depth of human experience. Listen to their accomplishments, their challenges and joys. This is our transgender, our human existence.

Please note that client names have been changed to protect their privacy.

Sarah's Story of the Power of a Name
Sarah, a bright teenager, faced daily battles with her self-identity, feeling trapped in a body that didn't mirror her soul. One of her most significant challenges was her struggle with her name, which was given to her at birth but didn't resonate with who she was. Sarah's relief came when she courageously approached her parents, discussing the importance of a name and how it affected her mental health. With understanding and time, her family embraced the change, signaling their acceptance and support.

David's Tale Beyond Stereotypes
David, an athletic and effervescent young man, often confronted stereotypes about how a transgender man should look and behave. People expected him to renounce his love for fashion, art, and dance. David's triumph was in his refusal to be boxed in. He continued to embrace his

passions, teaching his peers and family that gender identity and personal interests aren't mutually exclusive.

Anita and Raj, Parents on a Journey

Anita and Raj, parents to a transgender son, initially grappled with their own preconceptions, cultural pressures, and fears for their child's future. However, their love for their son propelled them to seek knowledge, attend support groups, and engage in open dialogues with their child. Their success was in the creation of an accepting home; fostering an environment where their son could thrive authentically.

Nina's Leap of Courage

Nina grew up in a tight-knit, traditional community where gender norms were strictly defined. From an early age, she knew she was different but felt constrained by her surroundings. After years of internal turmoil and self-doubt, Nina decided to pursue her truth. She relocated to a city known for its diverse and accepting community. Using social media, she reached out to a local non-profit organization for housing and employment assistance. Her victory wasn't just in finding herself but also in starting a community group back in her hometown to support other transgender youth; making sure they had a safe space she once yearned for.

Eli's Professional Challenge

Eli was a respected educator in his local school district. When he transitioned, he faced misunderstandings and prejudice. Some parents even questioned his capability as a teacher. But with the support of the principal and several colleagues, Eli launched school-wide educational sessions about gender identity and transgender topics. He witnessed the school community's transformation from apprehension to understanding and acceptance. However, it wasn't until his students, held in his honor, a thank you ceremony for being a beacon of light, for not just transgender students but also the LGBTQIA2S+ community, that he began to grasp the magnitude of his work's impact.

Lucia and Javier: Love Beyond Labels

Lucia and Javier were childhood sweethearts. When Lucia shared her truth, that she was a trans-feminine; it posed a challenge for their relationship. Faced with societal judgments and their personal apprehensions, the couple undertook couples therapy. With time, a willingness to adjust their expectations, and a lot of honest communication, they navigated through the complexities. Over the course of this 2 year period, with consistent couples and group counseling, they strengthened bond, and eventually became advocates for other couples on similar journeys.

Aria's Quiet Transformation

Aria, unlike many, had the support of her family from day one. However, she faced her battles in silence, notably body dysphoria. Without drawing much attention, Aria began her transition, seeking medical and psychological support. While a few noticed the visible changes, none understood the quiet battles Aria faced daily. Her victory was in her resilience, fighting silent battles with dignity, and emerging stronger with each day. She chose to acknowledge that she might not feel good 100% of the time. With this, she accepted that by simply honestly acknowledging her feelings was her way of honoring herself. This, to Aria, was all she needed to feel complete.

Caleb's Musical Journey

Caleb had a voice that could move mountains. But as he transitioned, his voice began to change, and he feared he would lose his gift. Facing both identity and professional challenges, Caleb decided to adapt. He took voice training lessons, learned new techniques, and embraced his new vocal range. His triumph resounded in auditoriums and theaters, proving that change, even if feared, can bring about beautiful new beginnings. The key is to remain flexible and continue searching for possible solutions to the challenges on your path.

The nuances of life offers a multitude of experiences. Each story, whether it's a tale of challenge, transformation, love, or self-discovery, adds yet another unique frequency to the healing vibrations of the transgender journey. Embracing these narratives helps to forge connections, where we understand each other's struggles, and most importantly, celebrate the human spirit.

Each story, each challenge faced, each triumph celebrated, teaches us something invaluable. While we might not attune to their exact frequency, however, understanding their journeys provides insights into the broader transgender experience. We witness that each of us face challenges on our perspective paths, and as a result, develop unique frequencies designed by our manifested reality. We all contribute to the master Song of Existence itself.

Reflective Questions:

1. Can you recall a personal story or scenario where you faced challenges related to understanding gender? How did you overcome it?
2. What emotions arise when you hear stories of transgender individuals confronting and overcoming obstacles?

3. If you were in Sarah, David, or the parents' shoes, how do you imagine you'd react? What steps would you take to ensure understanding and acceptance?

Family Exercise: Role Reversal

Objective: Enhance empathy and understanding of transgender experiences by stepping into another's shoes.

Instructions:
1. Setup: Gather in a comfortable space. Ensure everyone feels safe to express themselves.
2. Activity: Choose one of the stories above or create a hypothetical one. Each family member takes on a role from the story.
3. Discussion: Engage in a role-play scenario, acting out potential dialogues and situations. After the role-play, discuss the feelings experienced, challenges perceived, and what they learned from the activity.
4. Closure: Conclude by reinforcing the idea that empathy and understanding are critical in navigating the complexities of gender identity. Encourage family members to use this exercise as a foundation to approach real-life scenarios with compassion.

Understanding the lives and experiences of transgender individuals isn't about surgeries and appearances. It's about heartbeats, breaths, tears, laughter, and most importantly, love. As we journey together, let's embrace every story, for they are the mosaic of our collective human experience.

CHAPTER 19: MOVING FORWARD: CULTIVATING A RESPECTFUL AND INCLUSIVE TOMORROW

An in-depth journey of understanding, acceptance, and empowerment, specifically regarding the transgender community, is a continuous one. As I sit here, reflecting upon the heart-heavy stories, challenges, and victories we've explored together, there's a clear realization that emerges, one of love, understanding, and hope.

It's essential to cultivate an environment for our children where empathy and inclusion aren't just buzzwords but deeply imbued values. The University of Wisconsin-Madison led a study that helped to explain the callous and impulsive antisocial behavior exhibited by individuals willing to commit crimes of hate for their personal beliefs. According to different brains scans, it revealed marked reduced connections between the parts of the brain responsible for feelings such as guilt and empathy[50]. As teachers, parents and guardians, our children often look to us as their compass, drawing from our behaviors, values, and teachings. And as a spiritual guide, having navigated the waters of both transgender experiences and spirituality, I believe the core of these teachings is rooted in respect, love, compassion, communication, and understanding.

Building a World on Empathy

Empathy, the simple yet influential act of putting oneself in another's shoes, is the foundation of understanding. Encourage your children to ask questions, understand diverse experiences, and always approach things with

---

[50] Pujara M, Motzkin JC, Newman JP, Kiehl KA, Koenigs M. Neural correlates of reward and loss sensitivity in psychopathy. Soc Cogn Affect Neurosci. 2014;9(6):794-801. doi:10.1093/scan/nst054

an open heart. It's not about agreeing with every perspective but understanding them.

Celebrating Differences

As community leaders we hold an incredible amount privilege and responsibility to shaping our children's worldview. One of the most invaluable lessons we can impart is the beauty of diversity. The world is a kaleidoscope of cultures, identities, experiences, and expressions. Each color, each shade, has its place, making the collective manga a true page turner. By teaching our children to embrace and celebrate diversity, we not only equip them for a globalized world but also help them develop empathy, understanding, and respect for all individuals, regardless of their backgrounds or identities.

The 2025 year observed the United States of America, led by hateful Republicans and their nationalist religious leader, rescind all protections for transgender minors' rights to medical care. Transgender and non-binary people were, by law, to be criminalized if they used public bathrooms that did not align with the gender assigned at birth. Executive orders to remove all federally supported Diversity, Equity, and Inclusion programs were signed. Laws were implemented to punish not only educational staff, but also entire school districts, if "transgenderism" of any kind is supported by a school official or mentioned in the classroom. This is modern genocide, definitive actions taken to single out, discriminate against, falsely imprison, and eventually eradicate an entire minority group, the transgender community.

The topic of gender, particularly transgender identities, is an important facet of the diverse human experience. Children are naturally curious and perceptive. They will notice differences and will have questions about them. Instead of shying away from these discussions, we should welcome them as opportunities to educate and enlighten. By introducing our young ones to the many experiences of transgender individuals, we effectively dismantle myths and misconceptions, replacing them with accurate historical knowledge and truth. Books, films, and stories that feature transgender characters or themes can be invaluable tools in this endeavor, allowing children to see the world from diverse perspectives and recognizing that we have more things in common than different.

Celebrating diversity is about following your true passion and unapologetic living. One needs not to live out loud. Not everyone is meant to be in the public eye and that is OK. Our responsibility must first be to ourselves. To live happily and confidently. As leaders, our actions, conversations, and relationships act as live demonstrations of our beliefs. When we can stand on truth, embrace diverse friends, challenge prejudiced comments, and attend cultural events different from our own, we silently convey a message to our children. We tell them that diversity isn't just something to be tolerated but celebrated, that every individual, regardless of their gender identity, race, religion, or nationality, brings something special to the table, something worth cherishing and learning from.

The Power of Words

Words stand as potent tools that possess the ability to shape realities, evoke emotions, and bridge divides. The phrases we utter and the language we use have implications that go beyond mere communication; they form the very energetic material of our interpersonal connections and societal structures. Words, with their subtle tones and powerful connotations, can either uplift spirits and forge understanding or perpetuate prejudices and sow discord. As such, it is imperative to recognize and harness their strength, especially when introducing our children to the sensitive topic of transgender identities.

When discussing the subject of transgender people with young minds, the language we employ is highly important. Terms that are affirming and respectful can foster a safe environment where children feel empowered to ask questions, share feelings, and cultivate empathy. Conversely, derogatory language or even unintentional misgendering can perpetuate misunderstandings and inadvertently teach children that it's acceptable to disregard or belittle another's identity. This is why it's crucial to educate ourselves about the correct terminologies and phrases associated with the transgender community. When children witness their role models, the coaches, instructors, or parents, using language respectfully and conscientiously, they internalize the importance of words and their potential impact on others.

Yet, beyond the mechanics of language, there's a deeper lesson to impart about the essence of words. It's vital for children to understand that words carry with them the weight of human history, human emotions, and human experiences. When we speak about someone's gender identity, we're discussing a foundation aspect of their Being, their journey, and their truth. Teaching our kids to choose their words wisely helps them to develop awareness of their verbal power, their own magic. The power of words, when harnessed correctly, can be the light that guides us back to respect and understanding in a world that deeply needs it.

A Lifelong Journey

Transitioning is not a singular event, nor is it a fleeting moment that comes and goes like the changing seasons. It is a continuous unfolding, an alignment with one's inner truth that evolves over time. For transgender and non-binary individuals, this journey is lifelong, shifting in ways that reflect their growth, self-discovery, and the experiences that shape them. Just as the bodies of the solar system move in cycles, never stagnant, so too does a person's understanding of their identity. Some may begin with social changes like names, pronouns, and presentation, while others may explore medical or spiritual paths to further affirm who they are. No matter the direction, the transition is not a phase, but a sacred path of becoming.

For parents and guardians, adjusting to this reality requires patience, openness, and a willingness to listen without judgment. The most powerful gift they can offer is the assurance that love is unwavering, even as identities and expressions shift. Create a home that welcomes open dialogue, where questions and emotions can be shared without dismissal.

As a child, I can distinctly remember asking questions about gender roles and being shut down and told that religion was the path; and if I wanted to get right with their deity, then I need to pray away the desire to "seek knowledge" if I wanted to avoid going to hell. Each time I was told this, because it was definitely more than once, I was always left in a great state of confusion. I would follow up with, "How will I know if I don't ask?" However, around the young and impressionable age of 11, I found myself seeking comfort from unsavory character or other ill-educated adults; which placed me in very vulnerable and dangerous situation. Only after arriving well into my adulthood did I begin healing from my traumatic upbringing. That journey was initiated when I discovered my authentic community and took the frightening first-step to reach out and ask for help. Every stage of recovery confirmed that I had the resilience and power to find foundational answers and comfort from within. Discovering my authentic self-led to walking in my truth as a transgender man. I am continuously growing and learning more about my body, my mind, and my spirit.

Recognizing that there is no "final destination" in becoming your true self can help families to remain flexible and supportive, embracing each stage as it comes. This highlights how critical it is for friends and family to provide not just passive tolerance, but active affirmation.

Support does not always mean having all the answers. It can be as simple as sitting beside a child when they feel lost, standing up for them in spaces where they feel unseen, or honoring their journey even when it differs from what was expected. Just as the Virgo Cluster spans millions of lightyears, so too must love stretch beyond preconceived notions, making space for the infinite possibilities of identity. A lifelong journey is not meant to be walked alone, and when caregivers choose to walk alongside their transgender and non-binary child with open hearts, they become part of something far greater than themselves; an enduring legacy of love, acceptance, and belonging.

Reflective Questions:

1. How do I currently respond when confronted with concepts or identities I don't immediately understand? What can I do better?
2. How can I lead by example in showcasing inclusivity to my children?
3. In what ways can I incorporate learning about diverse stories and identities into our daily lives?

Family Exercises: Cultivating Inclusion

Objective: This activity helps family members empathize with the experiences of transgender individuals, emphasizing the emotions and challenges they might face.

Instructions:

1. Transgender Timeline: Create a timeline together as a family. Place significant events, pioneers, and milestones related to transgender history on it. This activity not only educates but also shows the long, affluent history of transgender individuals.

2. Pronoun Practice: Dedicate a day where everyone in the family tries using they/them pronouns. It's a small, simple exercise that can make everyone understand the importance of correct pronoun usage and how it feels.

3. Story Sharing: Allow each family member to share a story or experience where they felt different or out of place. It can be a stepping stone to discussing how transgender individuals often feel in society and the importance of understanding and acceptance.

In closing, remember that every conversation you have, every question you answer, and every story you share brings us one step closer to a world that understands, accepts, and celebrates all its beautiful differences. Let's move forward, hand in hand, heart to heart, towards a brighter, more inclusive tomorrow.

CONCLUSION

EMBRACING AUTHENTICITY IN A DIVERSE WORLD

As we come to the close of this enlightening journey, let's pause for a moment and reflect on the path we've traveled together. I hope that the lessons shared and the stories told have provided a deeper understanding of the amazing mosaic of gender diversity, not only as abstract concepts but as lived realities.

Being a black transman, my experience intertwines the complex layers of race, my masculinity, gender, and spirituality. Yet, this intersectionality isn't a burden. Instead, it provides an unaltered lens to see the world, a viewpoint that blends the ancestral wisdom of my African roots with the liberating journey of gender self-discovery. This is a journey filled with challenges, no doubt, but also resplendent with moments of joy, love, and deep realization.

In many ancient cultures, those who straddled the boundaries between male and female were well-regarded, seen as individuals with exceptional spiritual gifts. They were believed to possess an elevated understanding of the human experience because they lived at the confluence of dual energies. I believe this perspective still holds truth today. Our identities can act as bridges, connecting different communities, and fostering mutual understanding.

The spiritual teachings I've leaned on throughout my journey have consistently pointed to one truth: At our core, we are all interconnected. Whether you believe in a higher power or simply in the power of human connection, the principle remains. When we strive to understand and embrace one another, irrespective of our backgrounds or identities, we tap into a beautiful, shared humanity.

Children, with their natural curiosity and lack of prejudice, are especially open to understanding the complexities of gender. As guides, parents and guardians, you play a fundamental role in nurturing this curiosity, ensuring it grows into genuine understanding and empathy. By introducing them to the valued world of gender, you are preparing them for a diverse and inclusive future.

As you move forward, let the insights from this book serve as a foundation. I invite you to keep an open heart, always willing to learn, and always willing to teach. Remember, true enlightenment doesn't come from simply understanding oneself but from understanding and embracing the countless souls that share this world with us.

In this multiverse of energetic abundance, there's a teaching that resonates deeply with me:

The light in me honors the light in you.

It's a simple yet thoughtful acknowledgment of our shared divinity and humanity. By seeing and honoring the light in others, we illuminate our own path and the world around us.

Thank you for sharing this journey with me. I hope that this book has been a source of illumination, understanding, and inspiration, propelling you and your loved ones towards a future where every individual is cherished for their authentic self.
In Closing,

Let Us Be Present.

Let Us Be Of Light.

Let Us Be Of Love.

~*Liam*

ABOUT THE AUTHOR

Liam J. Adair is a beacon of inspiration and hope in the realms of holistic health and spiritual wellness. As the first black Transgender Holistic Healthcare Practitioner in the United States of America, Liam's journey has been one of resilience, self-discovery, and true dedication to the well-being of others.

Born and raised amidst the lush energy of cultures and wisdoms, Liam's life was always guided by an innate quest for knowledge and understanding. His experiences, both challenging and enlightening, led him to bridge the gaps between traditional practices and contemporary needs, particularly for those within the transgender and non-binary community.

Liam's teachings are not just rooted in ancient wisdom but are also backed by modern-day science and empirical research. He seamlessly merges the spiritual with the practical-using his nutritional and spiritual programs-providing guidance that's both astonishing in its depth and applicable in its approach.

Beyond his professional achievements, Liam's true essence lies in his advocacy for transgender rights, equitable healthcare, and his endeavor to dispel myths and misconceptions surrounding gender diversity. He believes that at the core of holistic health lies the need for acceptance, both self-acceptance and the acceptance of others, in all their beautified manifestations.

Today, as an author, speaker, and healing facilitator, Liam J. Adair continues to touch lives, encouraging all to dance with the spirits, listen deeply to the universe's whispers, and walk the path of understanding and love.

OTHER LITERARY WORKS BY: LIAM J. ADAIR

Novels and Course Books:

- Crystal Healing For Your Chakras: The TRUE Call of Nature; A Beginner's Guide to the World of Healing Crystals, 2019
- Fear Rules My Life: How to Develop & Use Your Personal Power to Overcome & Conquer Your Fears, 2020
- Walk in Your Truth: Unlocking the Authentic You: Wellness Life Coaching Course Workbook, 2022
- 14 Gemstones of Anxiety: How to Create a Crystal Layout for Anxiety with a Focus on Acupuncture Points, 2023
- Flourish to Authenticity Wellness Life Coaching Workbook for Holistic Health, 2023
- Healing Harmonies: A Guide to Soundbaths, Workshop, 2023

Activity Books:

- Adult & Teen Coloring Book for Anxiety and Stress Relief: Attain Mindfulness and Relaxation and Color Your Way to Peace, 2022
- LGBT Word Search for Adults and Seniors (Large Print), 2022
- Adult Coloring Book for Relaxation: Beautiful Mandala and Paisley Pattern Birds, Butterflies, Dragonflies, and More. 2022
- Mandala Adult Coloring Book: Beautiful Mandala Stress Relieving Designs for Adult Relaxation, 2022
- Fairies & Unicorns: Line Art Adult Coloring Book, 2022
- Princess and Unicorns Coloring Book for Kids Ages 4 – 12, 2023
- Adult Coloring Book of Magnificent Animals for Mindfulness Volume I: Adult and Teen Coloring Book for Stress Relief and Relaxation, 2023
- Adult Coloring Book of Magnificent Animals for Mindfulness Volume II: Adult and Teen Coloring Book for Stress Relief and Relaxation, 2023
- Easter Coloring Book for Kids Ages 3 to 8, 2023
- Halloween Coloring & Activity Book for Kids Ages 4- 12: Volume 1 - 3, 2023
- The Coloring Book of Phenomenal Dragons: Stress Relief Coloring Book for Adults and Teens, 2023
- Swear Words From Around the World Adult Coloring Book: Funny Curse Words and Dirty Adult Language, 2023
- Dream Journal Self-Care Monthly Planner, 2023
- LGBTQIA2S+ History Word Search: Large Print, 2023
- Adult & Teen Coloring Book for Anxiety and Stress Relief: Attain Mindfulness and Relaxation and Color Your Way to Peace, Vol. II 2024

www.ingramcontent.com/pod-product-compliance
Lightning Source LLC
Chambersburg PA
CBHW050522100526
44581CB00002B/73